Prayer and Common Sense

Thomas H. Green, S.J.

Prayer and Common Sense

AVE MARIA PRESS
Notre Dame, Indiana 46556

Imprimi Potest:	Rev. Noel D. Vasquez, S.J.
	Provincial Philippine Province
	October 1, 1994
Nihil Obstat:	Monsignor Socrates B. Villegas
	Vicar General
Imprimatur:	Jaime L. Cardinal Sin
	Archbishop of Manila
	October 4, 1994

International Standard Book Number: 0-87793-553-X
0-87793-551-3 (pbk)

Library of Congress Catalog Card Number: 95-75316

Cover design by Elizabeth J. French

Printed and bound in the United States of America.

Contents

Introduction

Taking Stock

The story is told that a famous and famously obscure poet (was it Ezra Pound?) was once asked what his poetry meant. He replied, "It means precisely what it says. If I meant something else, I would have said something else!" Whatever the merits of such a put-down in the realm of deep poetry, it certainly would not do in the case of my own writing on spirituality. My whole purpose is to make clear, intelligible, and relevant to my readers the admittedly mysterious ways in which God works.

I am, by temperament and vocation, a teacher and not a research scholar. I teach in the Philippines where, I have learned, Filipinos talk with their eyes. I must keep constant eye contact with my students in order to be sure I am making sense to them. At times I see that I am not, and in that case we have to back up and try again — perhaps using another analogy or approaching the topic in a different way. With you, my readers, eye contact is not possible; but ear contact is.

For example, the book which readers most often tell me they have found helpful but difficult is *Weeds Among the Wheat*, on discernment. Over time I have learned to suggest that they begin with Chapter 3, which is concrete and personal and practical. Chapters 1 and 2 give the biblical

background of discernment. They are important, since all
of our faith must ultimately be grounded on scripture; but
for many people it seems more helpful to read them after
Chapter 3. In fact, that is the order I now follow in my
course on discernment and spiritual direction.

Another difficulty for my readers is seeing the unifying
threads among my various books (now eight in number)
and knowing where they should begin. I have tried not to
write the same book twice. In my mind, each one answers
a different question, tackles a different aspect of the life of
contemplation and action. They can be grouped, however,
under three headings.

The first group would include those that deal with the
dynamics of formal prayer. *Opening to God* (1977) treats of
the beginnings of a good prayer life. *When the Well Runs
Dry* (1979) is concerned with "prayer beyond the beginnings," specifically with the struggle to accept the dryness
which St. John of the Cross tells us is itself contemplation
and is the normal lot of anyone who perseveres in a life of
listening prayer. Finally, *Drinking From a Dry Well* (1991)
asks what happens — what God is doing and how we can
cooperate best — after we have come to be at home in the
dry darkness of contemplation.

A second grouping would include the two books which
treat discernment explicitly. *Weeds Among the Wheat* (1984)
is my attempt to explain and apply to contemporary culture the classic rules of St. Ignatius Loyola for discerning
God's will in the choices we have to make in life. When I
wrote *Darkness in the Marketplace* three years earlier (1981),
I was, without quite realizing it, laying the foundation for
my later discussion of the "mechanics" of discernment. As
I see it now, *Darkness* is really asking what sort of person
one must be — what sort of faith-vision of life and experience one must have — in order to be able to discern the
Lord's will. From this perspective, *Darkness in the*

Marketplace is a much more extended and discursive presentation of the topic of Chapter 3 of *Weeds Among the Wheat.*

Finally, I would group together the other three books under this rubric: they discuss the link between formal prayer and discernment in various specific life-situations which I encounter in my ministry. *A Vacation With the Lord* (1986) is my interpretation and adaptation to today of the *Spiritual Exercises* of St. Ignatius Loyola. It is the only one of my books which first appeared in audio-cassette form. While I spent two or three months revising the transcript of the cassettes, the book retains the same format and purpose. It is intended to be lived and not merely read. It is a "guidebook" for one who wishes to actually make the Spiritual Exercises.

By contrast, *Come Down Zacchaeus* (1988) attempts to situate prayer and discernment within the context of the lay vocation. It is based on my conviction that the central thrust of Vatican II, from the Holy Spirit's point of view, was to bring the church into the age of the laity — and to bring the laity to the realization that they are not second-class Christians; that, as the Council says, they too are called to holiness just as much as are priests and religious.

Prayer and Common Sense fits into this third grouping of books on the relationship between discernment and everyday life. If *Vacation* focuses on a particular activity — making a retreat, and *Zacchaeus* on a particular state of life — the lay, this new book could be said to focus on one particular and extremely important quality of any genuine life of prayer and discernment — common sense. My conviction is that, despite the rigidity and intolerance of many devout persons in almost every spiritual tradition, God is really the most sensible person I know. Anyone who is truly growing in holiness should be becoming more like God, more sensible. In this new book I try to work out the meaning and the implications of that conviction. It is not surprising that beginners might find God arbitrary and unpredictable. But this should be less so as we mature in prayer and life, as we ourselves acquire "the mind of Christ." In attempting to show this, I begin from my own early experience. While this is personal, it is also, I believe, rather typical — not in its specific details, but in the gradual transition to a more "sensible" spirituality which I discern in my own life.

I am often asked this: "Where should I begin in reading your books?" My answer is that it depends on what the questioner is looking for. If your main concern is to grow in prayer, or to learn how to pray, I would suggest beginning with *Opening to God*, and then continuing with the other two books on prayer, insofar as they seem to speak to your own prayer experience thus far. If your concern is to discover God's will in the decisions that confront you, or to see God's meaning in the trials you are facing, my suggestion would then be to begin by reading *Darkness in the Marketplace*. And finally, if you have a specific question concerning the link between prayer and discernment, you might begin with whichever of the three books in the last group above seems most relevant to your question; although even here, *Darkness in the Marketplace* might be a helpful starting point.

When I write a book, I usually have to get away from San Jose Seminary (and especially from the telephone) in order to concentrate my energies on the task at hand. My Philippine Jesuit provincial, currently Fr. Noel Vasquez, S.J., and my rector at San Jose, Fr. Joel Tabora, S.J., have both been most gracious in giving me the time and space for writing. In the past I wrote at my mother's apartment. Since she died in 1990, as I was finishing *Drinking From a Dry Well*, this time I stayed at McQuaid Jesuit High School in my hometown, Rochester, New York. The

Jesuit community and the superior, Fr. Frank McNamara, could not have been more welcoming. The guestmaster, Fr. Fred Betti, made me feel right at home, as did the president of McQuaid, Fr. Jim Fischer, who even offered me the use of his 1979 Monte Carlo. Fr. Dave Stump, the computer wizard of the school, provided me with a computer for my editing (I still do the first draft in longhand), and the office personnel — especially Arlene Brown, Anne Coyne, Judy DiCesare, and Tom Shields — were most helpful with the photocopying and other tasks.

I owe a special word of thanks to Fr. Tom McManus, a friend of forty-five years and my next door neighbor at McQauid, for proofreading the first computer printout and for many other day-by-day favors. Apart from my Jesuit brethren, I am also indebted to John J. Considine, Jr., my cousin; to Robert Hamma, my editor at Ave Maria for this book; as well as to Frank Cunningham, my publisher and loyal friend since my book writing days began in 1976; and to my two critical readers for all the books since 1976: Sr. John Miriam Jones, S.C. of Cincinnati, and my sister, Pidge James of Des Moines. I always said my mother was my most supportive reader, while Sr. John and Pidge, by reading with critical eyes, reassured me that the manuscript (while never perfect, of course) was safe to put before the world. They filled that role again, but they also provided all the support and encouragement which even my mom could have wished.

Finally, I have to dedicate this book to my mom and dad — since they, as they grew older, taught me most of what I needed to know about the common sense of the true friends of God. But I would also like to include in the dedication two of my aunts — among the many with whom I have been blessed — who have played a special part in my own growth in good sense. Ida Parkes is my father's only sister, and Genevieve Mooney is the widow of my mother's second brother. Ida and Gen are both in their 80s now. And both are aging with true gracefulness, embodying the common sense of God of which I speak in this book in their own unique ways and according to their own very different personalities. If I live into my 80s, I hope and pray I can do as well as they have done.

Part 1

The
Quest
for
Holiness

Chapter 1

What Holiness Is (and Is Not)

In the Christian context, what does it mean to be holy? The word is often used — usually of particular persons, some publicly known, like Mother Teresa of Calcutta, but others from our circle of immediate acquaintances. In any case, the meaning seems rather vague. At the most superficial level it can mean simply "pious" or "devout," those who wear their religion "on their sleeve" and speak of God or the will of God, in every sentence they utter.

Most truly religious people, however, realize that holiness must go deeper than mere patterns of language and pious modes of behavior. They are too aware of Jesus' conflicts with the Pharisees to identify external religiosity with true holiness. They know too well that *pharisaical* has come to denote religious hypocrisy in our language. So they mean something deeper, more authentic, when they call a person holy. Perhaps they mean close to God, truly and interiorly dedicated to a life centered on the Lord, more like Jesus himself than like the Pharisees.

This certainly brings us much closer to the Christian meaning of holiness. But it is still rather vague and general. What precisely characterizes one who is close to God? What does it mean, concretely, to live like Jesus and to share his passion for God's will? And how does one get to be such a person?

My Novitiate Experience: A Goal to Be Achieved

To begin with the last question, my own ideas of how one achieves holiness have changed radically in the last forty-five years. When I was a Jesuit novice in 1949-51, I saw holiness as the achievement of a strong will and a real commitment to ascetical renunciation of "the world, the flesh and the devil."

Such an ideal of holiness both attracted and repelled me. It seemed at various times — and occasionally at the same time — both inhuman and superhuman. I was a reluctant candidate for the religious and priestly life. When I applied for the Jesuits in 1949, at the age of seventeen, I was at least half hoping I would not be accepted. I had a girlfriend and an NROTC scholarship for college and medical school. And yet no one — at least no other human being — was pressuring me to apply. The problem was, rather, that I could not escape the sense that God was calling me. I knew, and the novice master made it abundantly clear to me, that I was free to refuse the call. But I didn't want to do that either!

As I look back, the clue to the real meaning of holiness was already revealed in my dilemma. If anyone should have had an inkling that this was God's project and not my own, I was that person. But I did not take the hint for many years. Perhaps this was, in part at least, because the novitiate formation at that time reinforced my own mistaken ideas. The good novice was strong, self-denying, determined to pay any cost to possess the pearl of great price.

Our approach to prayer illustrates this well. We were 130 Jesuit novices, divided between two large study halls, in which each of us had a desk, and beside the desk a kneeler — a small plank raised about five inches from the floor.

We had to meditate for an hour every morning and for another half-hour in the afternoon. And we had to kneel the whole time.

The real purpose of this exercise, of course, was to get to know and love the Jesus whom we were encountering in the scriptures day by day. But in practice it became an endurance contest, a sort of supernatural survival of the fittest. Whatever the topic for the day, my aching knees soon became the focus of my attention. And since the study-hall arrangement allowed the novice master, or the novice placed in charge of us, to observe the whole group at one glance, anyone who dared to stand or sit would soon be called to account. "Brother, are you sick?" "Oh, no, Father." "But I noticed you were not kneeling during prayer." So we knelt and suffered — and presumably became stronger men in the process.

At first, at least as I remember it today, I found the whole process baffling and frustrating. I had never known the Jesuits before entering the novitiate. And I was not even sure what should be happening during my prayer time. Particularly frustrating was the fact that many of the men around me appeared so devout and recollected. I later learned that their inner state was not very different from my own, and that to many of them I appeared to be the devout one. But at the time, at least in the beginning, my only consolation seemed to be cursing them, one by one, for having found the treasure that eluded me.

As time passed, of course — after the first few months — I began to discover the real meaning of meditation. Christ became personally real to me, and the scriptures began to yield their riches. Then the girlfriend and the scholarship started to lose their hold on me. I began to realize, dimly, the beauties of the alternative path that was opening up before me. And yet, as I recall it now, I still saw the new way as a mountain to be scaled. It would be my life project, tackled "for the greater glory of God."

One other memory from those early years may make this clear. There were some novices among us who seemed to be ideal, the perfect novices. They did everything right, and they did it with total dedication and intensity. They were models of the "high seriousness" of the Victorian literary critics, as applied to the religious life. They were the ideal novices — at least to my eyes — who seemed to have achieved holiness at an early age.

Then, as the months passed, one by one they left the novitiate! How could that be? If the truly dedicated novices, the holy ones, could not persevere, what hope was there for the common run of mortals like myself? It took many years for me to solve that mystery. But as I see it now, the men I admired so much (and they were admirable) were trying too hard — trying to scale the mountain by their own intense effort. That is why they appeared so impressive. But in the end human nature rebelled. The effort to "do it for God," quickly and totally, was too much too fast. The timetable and the project were theirs, not the Lord's.

Although I did not realize it then, they were to help me learn a lesson St. Benedict had learned and taught fourteen centuries earlier. Originally a desert hermit, Benedict soon discovered that holiness is not in the rigorous asceticism and extreme renunciation of the stylites (flagpole-sitters, we might say) and other desert figures, but in common life; that is, holiness is in living an ordinary life, in a community of fellow-disciples, with extraordinary love.

Strangely enough, my early experience helped me much later to enjoy and to laugh at (since humor is pain turned inside out) Garrison Keillor's description of his own early religious experience. The "Sanctified Brethren" of Lake Woebegon were not so different, in their high seriousness and solemn striving, from what I had been as a novice. Nor were Keillor's Woebegon Catholics a totally different breed. After all, their parish was "Our Lady of Perpetual Responsibility"! Thus, it seems, Benedict's lesson has to be relearned in every age. There is a Pharisee, and a perfect novice, in every one of us.

What I Have Learned About Mistaken Ideals

As time passed and I found myself more at home in my new life, the demands of our studies also increased. High school had not been very demanding; I could do my homework for one class during the preceding one, and still cope quite well. In fact, though I was no athlete, I managed to be involved in many of the other activities the school had to offer without jeopardizing my class standing. Now, however, the competition and the demands were much tougher. After the new and shocking experience of failing a few quizzes and exams, I began to realize that previously I had been a big fish in a small puddle. Learning to swim in the open sea proved much more difficult.

I survived and adjusted, of course (otherwise I would not be writing this today!). But the process of adjustment was not easy. And, although I did not realize it at the time, it involved a reorientation of my values and ideals. Moreover, the challenge was not only in the area of studies. I also had to learn some hard lessons about love, human and divine.

The challenge of divine love that I faced is the topic of several of the books I have written. While I have been greatly enriched by the sharing of those whom I have been privileged to direct, there is no doubt that what I wrote earlier — and will write in the chapters to follow — about our love-relationship with God, had to come from, and ring true to, my own experience.

What may not have been so obvious is this: My experience of human love, of both its beauty and its limits, was an equally important part of the purification (as I would now see it) of my values and ideals. I realize now that this is implicit in the importance I gave to the metaphor of human love in the earlier books on prayer. That metaphor, I believe, is of universal value. But I also realize that each of us experiences it, and is purified by it, in a uniquely personal way.

My own experience was somewhat unusual and is probably no longer duplicated, thank God, in the lives of religious today. When I entered the Jesuits at seventeen, I had had a normal and quite active social life. I even thought I was in love. Perhaps that love could have matured into something deeper and more genuine. But — and this is where my story becomes atypical — at seventeen I suddenly found myself in an all-masculine environment. For the next seven years young women were an increasingly dim and distant memory for me. Occasional forays into the catechetical apostolate merely served to keep the memory alive. My real world was a world of young men my age.

And what of human love, human friendship, in this environment? Ideally, I think, it was seen as one of the things we renounced for the love of God. We had friends among our classmates, but "particular friendship" — any intimate, in-depth, "special" relationship — was taboo. As celibates, our only really close friend was to be Jesus Christ. In practice, though, this was easier said than done. We had all the affective needs and insecurities of late adolescence. I know I did. As I learned later, I am an extrovert and a strong "feeler" on the MBTI personality index. And after the rigors of novitiate I wrestled with the challenges of integrating true human friendship — deep and personal but not exclusive or possessive — into a life that was truly celibate, truly centered on God alone. Some of these men are still among my closest friends, and among God's greatest gifts to me, some forty years later. But finding the balance between the love of God and human love was a tricky and, at times, precarious experience in an environment that was hardly normal.

By the grace of God, though, I did learn my lesson. I came to realize that I can have many loves in my life, but only one center, and only one centering love. The other loves are good and holy as long as they are planets in my solar system and remain peacefully in their orbits around the one sun, Jesus Christ. One peculiar feature of my own experience is that by the time women re-entered my life — and I have been blessed with many women friends over the years — I had discovered and claimed my Center. They fell into their planetary orbits with relative ease and grace.

Today the situation of young seminarians is quite different. Many, perhaps most, begin their celibate lives at a more mature age, with a clearer picture of who they are and what they are seeking. The seminary situation is much more open and human. The seminarians have women as classmates, and they wrestle with the problems of intimacy in a more natural way. In fact, I often say jokingly that I have one gray hair for each of my seminarians who has fallen in love over the past twenty-five years. I am happy, though, that they can face the challenges realistically and discuss them openly with their directors before making a life commitment. My gray hairs, and by now they are many, are a small price to pay for this.

What, then, have I learned over the years? And what must all of us learn, despite our unique and diverse circumstances, about the road to holiness? In the first place, it is not my project but God's. It is not primarily a gift I give, or a goal I achieve, but a gift I receive. It is God's work almost totally. I say "almost" because we do have to do something. God stands at the door and knocks. And once the door is opened, God invites us in to share a meal

(Rv 3:20). But we must open the door; God will not force the invitation upon us.

How different this "opening to God" is from the ideal of holiness with which I began my religious life! Far from scaling the mountain of God with great personal effort and sacrifice, I have learned that what I have to do is to allow myself to be carried. Not that it is easy to do so. To let go of my own striving and learn to dance to the music of Another requires an asceticism even more demanding than that which broke the spirits of some of my co-novices. But it is a different kind of asceticism to which we are called, one of surrender rather than of achievement.

The scriptures echo this call, once we have the ears to hear it. Perhaps Paul, in his great treatise on grace and good works, expresses it most bluntly and clearly:

> It is the same justice of God that comes through faith to everyone, Jew and pagan alike, who believes in Jesus Christ. Both Jew and pagan sinned and forfeited God's glory, and both are redeemed by the free gift of his grace by being redeemed in Christ Jesus. . . . So what becomes of our boasts? There is no room for them. . . . since, as we see it, a person is justified by faith and not by something the law tells him to do (Rom 3:22-24,27-28).

So everything is gift. My real struggle at the beginning was not to earn the gift but to accept it, to allow God to give it to me. And to come to realize how truly and radically all is gift. "We were still helpless when at his appointed moment Christ died for sinful men and women," Paul proclaims. And "what proves that God loves us is that Christ died for us when we were still sinners" (Rom 5:6,8). The realization of its giftedness, its gratuitous quality, was perhaps the most important lesson I had to learn about holiness.

There were, however, other valuable lessons along the way. From my experience with my studies, I learned that

God's gift requires our active and sometimes intense cooperation. Receptivity is not pure passivity. Asceticism is needed, not to deny or despise human nature but to discipline it. Some years ago penance was seen almost as an end in itself, as a way to please God. In recent years a reaction has set in, and penitential practices are thought of, if they are thought of at all, as somehow dehumanizing — and certainly no way to please a good and loving God. The reaction is understandable, but we may have thrown out the baby with the bath water.

We will return to the topic of penance and asceticism in Part Two, when we discuss the common sense of God. Now, though, let me highlight the other important lesson about ideals and values of holiness which I had to learn. It is this: God is not found by denying our human loves and needs but by ordering them. My way of learning this was certainly messy and confused. Maybe that is the way for all human beings. But the lesson has to be learned. As St. John of the Cross puts it, all of creation is good. The problem is not with creatures but with our disordered attachment to them. My family, my girlfriend, my scholarship, and later, my friends in the Jesuits and my desire to do well and to accomplish great things for God — all of these were, and are, good in themselves. But, as St. Ignatius expresses it, they are means, not ends. The only end is the glory of God and my own salvation. All else is a means relative to this ultimate end.

I spoke about this teaching of John and Ignatius in relation to prayer in *Drinking from a Dry Well*. But it is a universal principle. And even in a healthier human environment than that of my novitiate, it is a very difficult principle to apply and to live. In fact, it is probably more difficult in a healthier environment. As I look back now, it seems we were trying to solve the problem by radical surgery, by radical denial. It was the baby/bath water syndrome again.

Today, we see the value of these human goods, and we seek to integrate them into our planetary system rather than to deny them. It is a much healthier and more godly approach, but it is definitely more difficult. That, after all, is why I have so many gray hairs!

What I Have Learned About What Holiness Really Is

We began this chapter with three questions about holiness. So far we have discussed the third: How does one get to be a holy person, close to God? We have seen that it is not a question of what we do ourselves, but of what we allow the Lord, with our active cooperation, to do in us. But our first question remains unanswered: What precisely does it mean to be holy, to be close to God? Or, in the scriptural rephrasing of our second question: What, concretely, does it mean to live like Jesus, sharing his passion for the Father's will?

This whole book is an attempt to highlight one very important but often neglected aspect of becoming more like Jesus, like God: experiencing and sharing God's common sense. But it will be helpful, first, to see the broad biblical picture of holiness. Here, as so often in my life of prayer and ministry, John McKenzie's *Dictionary of the Bible* provides a very helpful survey. Under the entry *holy* (pp. 365-67), McKenzie discusses both the Old Testament and the New Testament visions of holiness. (Also helpful are the following *Jerusalem Bible* footnotes: Lv 17a; Is 5i and 6h; Mk 1g; Acts 9g; 1 Cor 7b; and 1 Thes 4c.)

In the Old Testament the word *holy*, which has the basic meaning of "separate," is used primarily to signify God's very essence. McKenzie cites Rudolph Otto's famous analysis of the holy as the "numinous," the mysterious quality of being "wholly other," totally different from creatures. Unlike the gods of Greece and Rome, God is not just a super-human being, with both human virtues and failings writ large. Yahweh is totally unique, both physically and morally. Physically, it is dangerous, even fatal, for humans to approach God (recall the burning bush of Moses); the divine "glory" is the visible, physical manifestation of God's holiness. And morally, God's hidden holiness is manifested by his moral will, righteousness, judgment upon sin, and deliverance or salvation of the chosen people.

McKenzie gives numerous scriptural citations to illustrate each of the points he makes. What is important for us, however, is the overall picture. The holiness of the God of the Old Testament is this quality of being "wholly other," unique, totally different from and beyond the comprehension of creatures. In Otto's famous phrase, God is "*mysterium tremendum et fascinosum;*" at once repelling, "fearsome and tremendous," attracting, and fascinating. And the duty of the creatures is to proclaim God's holiness (being "wholly other"), and to refuse to reduce God, like the pagan gods, to their own creaturely level. In a word, they are to keep holy the "Name" which stands for the person of Yahweh.

From this magnificent perspective it seems almost blasphemous for us to aspire to holiness, to call mere men and women holy. And yet the Old Testament does apply the word to creatures, too. Here it means a quality "derived from the divine by some peculiar contact." As McKenzie describes it, the word is thus used primarily in a cultic and in a national sense. Most uses are cultic or liturgical, and this seems to be the primary creaturely meaning of holiness. The personnel and furnishings of the cult (and later the heavens, where God dwells; holy places, like Jerusalem and the burning bush; and even sacred seasons and sacrificial victims) are holy because of their unique association with the divine. In this cultic sense, the holy is contrasted with the profane — the latter referring to objects that are not evil but morally neutral, that can be used for any purpose.

Closely connected to the cultic sense of the word holy is its national sense. Israel is "the people holy to Yahweh." That is, she is worthy of, fit for the liturgical worship of God, because of her divine election. She is holy precisely because she belongs to Yahweh by election and by covenant (Ex 19:6; Lv 20:8; Dt 7:6). And she preserves her holiness not only by her worthy offering of cultic worship but by meeting the moral demands of Yahweh. Derivatively, we occasionally read that individuals are sanctified — made holy — usually for war, but in one striking instance (Jer 1:5) for a prophetic mission. On occasion, too, the road to Jerusalem is referred to as "the holy way" (Is 35:8); and the angels (Ps 89:6; Jb 5:1) and the spirit of Yahweh (Ps 51:13; Is 63:10) are called holy.

Thus the holiness of the Old Testament is primarily the wholly other quality of Yahweh. Creatures, and especially the people of Israel and the furnishings of her liturgical cult, participate in the holiness of Yahweh because of their special relationship to God. When we come to the New Testament, the same pattern of holiness is revealed, with certain striking differences or new emphases. As McKenzie notes, there are fewer references to the holiness of God, although we find noteworthy echoes of the Old Testament in the Our Father (Mt 6:9; Lk 11:2) and in Jesus' beautiful priestly prayer (John 17:11). Also, there are references to the Holy God in 1 John 2:20 and in Revelation 4:8 and 6:10.

Moreover, the holiness of creatures is still a participation in the holiness of God the Sanctifier. The cultic references to holiness (e.g., Mt 23:17-19; Heb 9:13) strongly echo the Old Testament Jewish tradition. But when we come to speak of the nation as holy, the new Israel, as we would expect, is the church. This is expressed with singular beauty in 1 Peter 2:9-10:

> But you are a chosen race, a royal priesthood, a conse-
> crated nation, a people set apart to sing the praises of
> God, who called you out of darkness into his wonder-
> ful light. Once you were not a people at all and now
> you are the People of God; once you were outside the
> mercy and now you have been given mercy.

Because of this union with God the Father, Christians are those who have been "sanctified" (Acts 20:32; 26:18), and are frequently called "the saints" (the "sanctified" or "holy ones") in Acts and in the epistles. The primary agent of their sanctification is God the Father, through Christ Jesus, in the Holy Spirit (1 Thes 5:23; 2 Thes 2:13; 1 Cor 1:30).

Thus in a real sense *every* Christian is holy by the very fact of baptism. The People of God, united in one baptismal faith, are a holy people. To call individuals holy in this sense is merely to affirm that God has called them out of darkness and set them apart to sing the divine praises. Merely, however, is scarcely the right word; this work of God in sanctifying us is our greatest glory and the founda-tion of all our hope.

The New Testament makes clear, though, that we cooperate actively in our sanctification. Thus, we might say, there are degrees of holiness in the Christian commu-nity, depending on the receptivity of the soil to the seed of God's gift (Mt 14:4-9). Baptism unites us with Christ, but faith is not only gift given but gift received. And we main-tain and deepen the holiness God has bestowed on us by avoiding sin (1 Cor 6:9-20) and by leading holy lives (2 Pt 3:11-14). So, it is meaningful to return to the question with which we began this chapter, to call certain persons holy in a special or distinctive sense. The problem, however — as we shall see in the next chapter — is that it is not easy to judge from externals the quality of a person's inner response to the gift of God.

Before turning to that question, let us complete our commentary upon McKenzie's presentation of the biblical notion of holiness. The angels, Jerusalem, the Temple and its furnishings, are all referred to in the New Testament, as in the Old, as holy. What is new is the insistence that all created reality can be "sanctified" by "the word of God and prayer" (1 Tm 4:4-5). The levitical distinction between the profane and the sacred no longer holds. All food, all creation, is good if it is ordered to the glorification of God. Was I, then, implicitly an Old Testament man in my novitiate years? It seems so to me now. I recall how we novices used to stand above the New York Central tracks along the Hudson River, watching the people in the dining cars of the Twentieth Century Limited as it passed by, and saying, half wistfully and half with conviction: "They are not really happy!" It seems we needed to believe that they were not in order to justify our life of renunciation. I might have been much more integrated, and happier, if I had been able to move into the New Testament earlier.

The Old Testament mention of individuals being sanctified for mission is also echoed in the New Testament. Hence Jesus, in his priestly prayer, asks that his apostles be "consecrated in the truth" (Jn 17:17-19). But now it is Jesus himself, above all, who is consecrated by the Father (10:36) and consecrates himself (17:19) for the mission of salvation. He is "the holy one of God" (Mk 1:24, among others) and "the holy servant of God" (Acts 4:27-30). He has a unique relationship of mission to the Father, to Yahweh.

For a Christian, to be holy is to put on the Lord Jesus, to live "now not with my own life but with the life of Christ who lives in me" (Gal 2:20). Christian holiness is a way of life, as it was in the Old Testament. But now this means not primarily a life of faithful observance of the law, but a life of loving intimacy with the Father, lived through, with, and in Jesus Christ. And it is the Holy Spirit whose indwelling presence in the disciple — a frequent and gradually clarified theme in Paul, Luke, and John — effects this sanctifying union with the God and Father of Jesus.

Thus the holiness of the Christian, from beginning to end, is primarily the work of the God of love. While the continuity of doctrine between the Old and New Testaments is striking, even more striking is the radical newness of the New Testament revelation. Vatican II's stress (*Lumen Gentium*, the Decree on the Church, chapters 4 and 5) on the universal call to holiness of all Christians, and especially of the laity, is a striking contemporary expression of this radical newness. Every Christian is holy by reason of baptismal consecration. And every Christian is called to grow in holiness. There are no class distinctions when it comes to the call to union with God in Christ Jesus.

In the next chapter I will suggest that we might do better to speak of people as loving, rather than as holy. This is because of the erroneous connotations which the word holy has acquired in our contemporary culture. But we must admit that the word has a rich and perfectly sound biblical basis, and that the New Testament ideal of holiness is best expressed precisely in Jesus' command to love as we are loved (Jn 13:34). We are no longer servants but friends (Jn 15:15). As I understand this beautiful passage, our ideal of holiness is no longer that of the good servant of the Old Testament. As New Testament women and men, we are called to be friends of the Lord and of one another, united to God by the bond of mutual love.

Chapter 2

Recognizing the Holy Person

What have we discovered thus far? That holiness is the vocation of every human being, and specifically of every disciple of Jesus Christ, and that this call to holiness is a call to love as we are loved. It is clearly not a question of external piety, which may well be good and genuine but, at its best, is only a manifestation of a deeper inner attitude toward and experience of God. Since we are human beings, our inner dispositions and values do need to be embodied, incarnated, in sensible ways. A man who professes to love his wife, but never shows it in his way of acting and speaking, is certainly suspect. On the other hand, glib talk and gallant behavior may mask a hollow and selfish heart.

Holiness, we have also seen, is not a bootstrap operation. We do not achieve it by our own efforts, although God does respect our freedom and await our cooperation. God makes us holy in baptism by calling us out of darkness into his marvelous light. And then, provided we cooperate, God brings to perfection the good work begun in us. Concretely, this means our learning to love as we were first loved: to "love the Lord your God with all your heart, with all your soul, and with all your mind," and to "love your neighbor as yourself. On these two commandments hang the whole Law, and the Prophets also" (Mt 22:37-40).

So the work is God's. In the most beautiful of the prayers of thanksgiving with which Paul begins virtually all his letters (Galatians being the striking exception), he tells the Philippians: " I am quite certain that the One who began this good work in you will see that it is finished when the Day of Christ Jesus comes" (1:6). At the same time Paul also stresses, even in this same letter (1:27 — 2:18), that it is necessary to "work for your salvation in fear and trembling." There is a dynamic tension at the very heart of our Christian faith, between insistence on the sheer gratuity of saving grace and stress on the importance of our good works in and for the kingdom of God. It is a tension, of course, which is already evident in Paul's own writings, when, for example, we read Romans 5 together with Romans 6. It is the balance I was struggling to achieve in the early years of my Jesuit formation.

Why Ask About My Holiness?

Having said all this, how do we know whether we are indeed growing in holiness, in union with God? To tackle a preliminary question first, why should we even care to know? Occasionally directees say to me: "I don't care what 'stage' of prayer I am in. That is too introspective, too self-centered. I just pray and love God — and leave the state of my soul, the stage I am in, to him."

The first time I had to face that question seriously was back in 1976. I was discussing the possible publication of *Opening to God* with the editors at Ave Maria Press. They suggested that I include some mention of pray-ers who simply pray, without any concern about methods and stages — whose relationship to God is quite spontaneous and uncomplicated. My first reaction was that such people, if they do exist, do not need my book or any book on prayer.

As I reflectèd further, however, and as other pray-ers posed the same challenge to me, I realized that things could never be that simple — at least on a permanent, long-term basis — in any genuine love relationship with the Lord.

As with human love, there can be periods of untroubled stability. At such times it may be best to leave well enough alone. But growth over time is never without its challenges and doubts. This was brought home to me most strikingly shortly before my mother died. I was in the Philippines, and something I read in the breviary (the Prayer of the Church, or Liturgy of the Hours, as it is called today) reminded me of my mom's relationship to my dad. He was the pious one, with a simple, quiet, unquestioning faith. She was the questioner. When I was young, in parochial school, I think I canonized my father and (to exaggerate slightly) worried about my mother's salvation.

On that day not long before her death, the reading in the breviary made me realize in a special way how good she had been for my dad. She was the life-loving extrovert and he the devout introvert. She was his link to the world. At this time he had been dead for about fifteen years, but she and I had corresponded weekly ever since I entered the Jesuits some forty years earlier. So that week I wrote to tell her my breviary insight concerning how good she had been for him. When she replied, and this is my reason for telling the story now, she said: "I was touched and gratified to read what you said about Dad and me. But one thing concerns me. Sometimes I fear that you kids think our relationship was too easy, too ideal. I hope you realize that even the best of marriages demands a great deal of dying on the part of both partners."

That was all she said. The message, though, came through to me loud and clear. I could see that it had to be true of any love relationship, even with God. As Jesus insisted (Mt 16:24-25), Gethsemane and Calvary are as essential to our story as to his. Moreover, the move from Tabor to Calvary cannot be serene and untroubled. We are bound to be disoriented, puzzled by the changing weather of our inner lives. If we are to respond gracefully to the Lord's evolving initiative, we have to be sensitive to what he is doing in us at the present moment. We need to know whether we are in step with the Lord of the Dance, in order to cooperate fully if we are, and in order to change our rhythm if we are out of step. We need, in short, to be discerning people. It is in this sense that it is important to know what "stage" we are in in our dance with the Lord.

The Difficulty in Reading the Signs

Fr. William J. Connolly, S.J., has an excellent monograph on "Contemporary Spiritual Direction: Scope and Principles" (June 1975 in the series *Studies in the Spirituality of Jesuits*, St. Louis University, Missouri). I use it in my course in Manila on discernment and spiritual direction, and the students find it most helpful. One of the points Fr. Connolly makes in discussing the work of the spiritual director is the importance of — and the difficulty of verifying —criteria to measure the growth of the directee (pp. 109-15). Such criteria are important to determine whether the director is really helping the directee to grow. St. John of the Cross is quite insistent that directors should try to possess the souls of directees. The director should always leave them free — indeed, should encourage them — to move on when someone else can be of more help to them.

This implies that directees should also be able to determine whether they are really growing in the present directorial relationship. Indeed, as I see it, the director is merely a co-discerner. The directees have primary responsibility for making this decision. They have to decide whether they are being helped to grow. The question for the directee, then, is this: How can I make this decision? Connolly says that the criteria, while essential, are difficult to verify in practice. External signs, like "adherence to law, good mental health, and conformity to the norms of the community," are helpful but not conclusive. A person can be law-abiding because she finds her security in the law. Another may be faithful to community schedules and spiritual exercises because he wants to appear good and to receive praise from others.

The real difficulty here, as Connolly notes, is that "the goal of the spiritual life is a deepening and increasing union with God, and that union itself cannot be objectively verified." The essential question is not whether the person is present at Mass and faithful to daily prayer, but whether he or she brings a truly open and listening heart to these activities. And how can we judge what is happening within a person? Here, I think, we have to make a crucial distinction between what the pray-er can see and what the director or outside observer can see. In some sense the pray-er, and only the pray-er, can observe what is happening within.

Even after my thirty-one years as a priest and a director, I can judge directees only by what they tell me of their inner dispositions and from their tangible, observable behavior. This is quite normal, but it does introduce a cautionary and humbling note into my work of direction. It is possible, if a directee is a good enough actor (or I a poor enough critic) that I can be mistaken for some time in my judgment of the person's state of soul. This is more likely to happen when I don't yet know a directee very well. In fact, I have come to the humbling realization that my first impressions, even of sincere and open directees, are often mistaken. This is not bad, provided I am wary of judging too quickly. If I approach direction with a more contemplative, listening heart — open to seeing what is really happening and not jumping to conclusions — it can be a beautiful voyage of discovery.

The situation of the directee is more properly our concern here. That is, we are asking how directees can judge that they are truly growing in their relationship to the Lord. They have the advantage that their inner attitudes and values are more directly accessible to them. They can look within. Even here, however, a healthy and humble caution is in order. That, after all, is why people come to me for direction. They are not sure how to interpret what is happening within. They feel they are not progressing, not growing. Or they think they see signs of real growth but are not sure whether they can trust their own judgment. I can be of help to them to the extent that I can assist them to interpret their own inner experience.

Pauline Criteria of Authentic Growth

Connolly's discussion of criteria of growth is helpful. He mentions first of all the marks of the Good Spirit, enumerated by Paul in Galatians 5:22: "love, joy, peace, patience, kindness, goodness, trustfulness, gentleness and self-control." These are helpful, indeed essential, signs of authentic Christian life in the Spirit. If any one, or more, of them seems to be lacking, we should be quite doubtful about the spirit of the person in question. Connolly notes, however, an important qualification: "The Pauline signs as they are listed appear to be absolute and perfected. They do not appear so in experience. Instead they appear in process of development, of sometimes unsteady growth" (p. 110).

What we seek are signs of genuine growth in the life of the Spirit, not proof that the person in question is already perfect, ready to be canonized. This may seem obvious, but I find that many directees judge their glass to be half-empty, when they should see it as half-full. After all, they started with an empty glass, and beginning with baptism, the Lord has been gradually filling it with divine life and love. We desire, as Paul did, to "have strength to grasp the breadth and the length, the height and the depth; until, knowing the love of Christ which is beyond all knowledge, (we) are filled with the utter fullness of God" (Eph 3:18-19). But that is eternal life — not our present situation — the goal of all our striving and of all God's work in us.

Since the goal is so magnificent, and so far beyond our natural human powers, we should expect that the process of attaining it will be slow and painstaking. In fact, as I get older I find that my impatience with the slow pace of my growth has given way to a different attitude. Now, considering the immensity of the transformation required to fill me "with the utter fullness of God," I marvel that the Lord can accomplish it in me in one short lifetime. Seventy years seems too short, not too long, for the work at hand.

But, the pray-er may ask, what if there seems to be no growth at all? What if I seem to struggle with the same failings year after year and confess the same sins month after month? This is where it is important to make a distinction, as I would express it, between sin as malice and sin as sickness. If the failings in question are deliberate (malice), and if I commit the same deliberate sins over and over again, then I should indeed question my growth — and my sincerity.

Not all our failings, however, are deliberate. There is also the situation of Romans 7, where "I fail to carry out the things I want to do, and I find myself doing the very things I hate" (vv 14-25). The situation Paul describes is not malice but sickness, a kind of spiritual schizophrenia, and is one I struggle with in my own life. As the commentators tell us, the "I" of whom Paul speaks is every human being. And in each of us, the victory is won "through Jesus Christ our Lord" (7:25). But, as Romans 8 makes clear, the tension persists even in those who have been reborn in the Spirit of Jesus. Why is this? Reflecting on my own experience and on that of my directees, I believe the Lord leaves these instinctual failings in us to keep us humble. They will be removed in God's own time. Apparently, though, God knows that we are not yet ready to be free — that we would be self-righteous and self-canonized if we were able to achieve total mastery of all our human instincts (sensuality, vanity, intolerance, etc.).

How then can we recognize growth in this area? If our sins of sickness do indeed make us more humble, more dependent on the grace of God to accomplish what is impossible to us, more tolerant of the failings of others, more willing to trust the Divine Physician (and hence to return to the sacrament of healing over and over again) for as long as the course of treatment takes — all these are the signs of growth which we seek. As is so often the case, Paul expresses it with powerful directness:

> To stop me from getting too proud, I was given a thorn in the flesh. . . . About this thing I have pleaded with the Lord three times for it to leave me, but He has said, "My grace is enough for you; my power is at its best in weakness." So I shall be very happy to make my weaknesses my special boast, so that the power of Christ may stay over me (2 Cor 12:7-10).

Because of this remarkable passage and its impact on my own life, I have often asked my retreatants: "Has it ever occurred to you to thank God that you are sick?" After all, Jesus himself said: "It is not the healthy who need the doctor, but the sick. I did not come to call the virtuous, but sinners" (Mk 2:17). If we are already virtuous before Jesus comes to us, we have no claim on him. Our very sickness is the guarantee that he came for us!

The Experience of Contemplation

This brings us to another, related criterion of true growth, which Connolly calls "the experience of Jesus." In speaking of the goal of spiritual direction, he also calls this

experience, or at least its peak moment, "contemplation."
He says that "the primary task of the director is to facilitate
contemplation." And he describes this contemplative attitude as happening when "the Lord readily becomes real
for him (the directee) and he readily lets himself be com-
pletely real with the Lord." This may be an unusual use of
the word *contemplation*, but it does point to a crucial turning point in every pray-er's life. I suppose for me, in my
novitiate, this happened when I finally discovered what
prayer was all about. It is a gradual process, of course, but
I am sure a day came when God, Jesus, was personally real
to me in an entirely new way. He was no longer an idea but
a friend, no longer "he" but "you."

Connolly's argument is that this turning-point moment
is a watershed in spiritual direction. Prior to this "God is
alive in my life!" experience, the director's role is to help it
to happen. Connolly says "the director must remember
what his primary task is, and help the directee to move
towards the contemplation that will be" (p. 115). Like John
the Baptist, I would say, the director's task is to call
directees to repentance — and to guide them to the
"places" where they may encounter Jesus. The director
does not seek to bind directees to himself or herself but
helps them search with clear and open eyes for the Beloved
whom they seek.

And when they find Jesus? What is the director's role
when Jesus, God, has become personally real to them? As I
see it, John the Baptist is still the best model for the director. John was the "friend of the Bridegroom," and the true
friend has enough sensitivity (*delicadeza*, we would say in
the Philippines) not to seek to go on the honeymoon. John
realized clearly that, at this point, "he must increase and I
must decrease" (Jn 3:28-30). The first disciples of Jesus all
had been disciples of John the Baptist. But once they left
everything to follow Jesus — not, as the gospels make clear,

without an occasional nostalgic glance backward at their former life with John — John knew that he must detach them from himself.

When my mother and my father married in 1931, they went to Bermuda for their honeymoon. In those days that meant an overnight train trip from Rochester to New York City, in order to board the cruise ship for Bermuda. My mom had two older brothers who were great practical jokers. They informed her and my dad that, since she was their only sister, they were going to accompany them on the honeymoon. My dad, who was quite serious and liked his jokes clearly labeled as such, was very apprehensive. My mom, who knew her brothers better, thought they were joking; but she was afraid that they were just "crazy" enough to do what they threatened. My uncles said they would leave the newlyweds alone on the train trip to New York but would meet them on the cruise ship. What a relief it was to both my parents when the gang-plank was lifted the next day and her brothers had not appeared!

It is important to note, though, that the director (the friend of the bridegroom or the bride) still has a role to play. There will be occasions in the pray-ers' new life of intimacy when they do not understand the behavior of the Bridegroom. Or when they do not understand their own behavior, their own reaction to unexpected situations in their ongoing relationship. At such times the director can be a trusted confidant and help them face the challenges more objectively and more peacefully.

I don't know whether my mother ever sought her brothers' advice. But I do recall her telling about the financial troubles she and my dad faced when the economic depression hit Rochester shortly after their marriage. Her own father was her confidant then, and he helped her to see that even losing their house (as they did) was not the end of the world. As long as she had a husband who truly loved her, he said, and as long as they could face their problems together, no external troubles were truly disastrous in the long run.

This is an excellent parable for the role of a good director, once the bride and the Bridegroom have begun their life together. The director is always available when needed, but does not interfere in the love relationship which is now the center of the bride's (the pray-er's) life. This is why, toward the end of the monograph to which I have referred, Connolly says that there is only one thing the director can "demand" of the directee: growth in freedom. The director cannot demand (or expect) that directees pray as the director prays, or have the same commitment to feminism or social justice or third-world liberation. Each person's relationship to the Lord is unique and personal. Good and holy as all these causes and prayer styles may be in themselves, only the Lord, the Bridegroom, can decide what he wants from this particular chosen friend of his.

All that the director can ask, then, is "a development of freedom, that is, that the directee move toward greater freedom to let the Lord be himself with him and to be himself with the Lord." Even here the choice is the directee's. But if the person is unwilling or unable to become more free, in the sense indicated, then the director should question whether their relationship is really of help. Maybe it should be terminated or, at least, shifted to another level, perhaps of simple friendship or of pastoral counselling. At the same time, growth in freedom is a good criterion for the directees to apply to themselves. If they find that they are becoming more authentically free — to simply be themselves, and to allow the Lord to be himself with them — then they can be confident that they are "growing in holiness."

Keeping Our Eyes on the Goal

From what we have seen thus far, it is clear that there is
a value in knowing where we stand on our journey with
the Lord. Only in that way can we cooperate fully with him
in the work of our sanctification. But there are problems
here. Whereas other people can judge us only by what they
see — can infer our interior attitudes only from the visible
fruits in our lives — we ourselves can see better what is
happening within us. And yet we know that it is quite possible to fool even ourselves. We know our own fickleness.
We are painfully aware of the sickness of Romans 7 within
us: our freedom is always mixed with and contaminated by
unfreedom. How then can we have any confidence that we
are on the right track in our quest for holiness?

It seems to me, based on all we have said, that the best
advice we can give directees is to keep things in proper
focus. The devil works to distort our vision, to make us lose
our focus on the Lord and his ways. With devout persons
the devil enters as an angel of light, suggesting ideas and
courses of action that appear good and holy but are really
not so. As St. Ignatius Loyola expresses it in his Rules for
the Discernment of Spirits (*Spiritual Exercises*, #332):

> It is a mark of the evil spirit to assume the appearance
> of an angel of light. He begins by suggesting thoughts
> that are suited to a devout soul, and ends by suggesting
> his own. For example, he will suggest holy and pious
> thoughts that are wholly in conformity with the sancti-
> ty of the soul. Afterwards, he will endeavor little by lit-
> tle to end by drawing the soul into his hidden snares
> and evil designs.

Can we apply this insight specifically to our discussion
of growth in holiness? It seems to me that there are three
areas here where the false angel of light seeks to distort our
vision — three areas which have surfaced in our present

discussion. To combat him, we need to focus on being "loving" rather than on being "holy"; on our process of growth rather than on our present state of perfection or imperfection; and, finally, on what we might call a "holy realism" in our growth towards perfect union with God. Let us say a word about each of these focuses.

At the end of Chapter 1, I suggested that it might be better to focus on love rather than on holiness, despite the fact that the words *holy* and *holiness* have a rich and solid biblical history. The problem is not with the authentic biblical usage, but with the connotations the words have when we use them of men and women today. During his ministry, Jesus wrestled with these connotations in his debates with the scribes and Pharisees. Only God is holy in the true and fullest sense of the word. Whatever holiness we possess is but a participation in his holiness, and is pure gift. Since we, like the Pharisees, are all too prone to appropriate for ourselves what is purely God's gift — and so to become self-righteous and even self-canonized — I think we would do better to focus on love and on being loving persons. At least I find that healthier myself. Since love by its very nature is self-giving and other-centered, there seems to be much less danger here of becoming preoccupied with my own self and my state of soul.

We saw at the beginning of this chapter that Jesus, when questioned by a scribe about the greatest commandment of the Law, replied that the whole Law and the Prophets (the Jewish way of referring to the Old Testament) is contained in the commands to love God with all our hearts, and to love our neighbor as ourselves. While all three of the synoptic gospels recount this incident, only St. Mark tells us the reaction of his questioner:

> The scribe said to him, "Well spoken, Master; what you have said is true: that he is one and there is no other. To love him with all your heart, with all your understanding

and strength, and to love your neighbor as yourself —
this is far more important than any holocaust or sacrifice.
Jesus, seeing how wisely he had spoken, said, "You are
not far from the kingdom of God" (Mk 12:32-34).

The beautiful reply of the scribe, and Jesus' commen-
dation of him, shows that he had grasped the central
importance of love in the life of the true disciple of Jesus.
And two incidents in St. Luke highlight the two essential
aspects of Jesus' law of love. In his inaugural discourse,
often referred to as the Sermon on the Plain, Jesus commands his disciples to love their neighbors, even (and particularly) their enemies.

> If you love those who love you, what thanks can you
> expect? Even sinners love those who love them....
> Instead, love your enemies and do good, and lend with-
> out any hope of return. You will have a great reward,
> and you will be children of the Most High, for he him-
> self is kind to the ungrateful and the wicked (Luke
> 6:32,35).

This teaching of Jesus makes very specific the command to love our neighbor. And in the following chapter
(7:36-50), he uses the incident of the public sinner, who
anointed his feet in Simon the Pharisee's house, to teach
Simon and us the meaning of wholehearted love for the
Lord. *The Jerusalem Bible* translates the crucial lines as fol-
lows:

> You gave me no kiss, but she has been covering my feet
> with kisses ever since I came in. You did not anoint my
> head with oil, but she has anointed my feet with oint-
> ment. For this reason I tell you that her sins, her many
> sins, must have been forgiven her, or she would not
> have shown such great love. It is the one who is forgiv-
> en little who shows little love.

A grateful love for the Lord, like the sinful woman's,

and a love which leads us to forgive our enemies because we have first been forgiven, fulfill the whole Law and the Prophets. That is where our energies should be concentrated. And if we are to speak of human holiness, let this be what we mean. There is no danger of vanity or self-delusion here. At the same time, from this perspective we see clearly the significance of the second focal point which I suggested: that is, to focus on our process of growth, rather than our present state of perfection or imperfection. Humanly speaking, love of our enemies, based on a grateful love that we ourselves have first been forgiven "when we were still his enemies" (Rom 5:7), is impossible to us. It makes no sense to demand of ourselves a perfection which only grace can accomplish in us, or to be proud of the extent to which we have achieved it.

Somewhere in his writings, the evolutionary or process philosopher John Dewey says that the good person is the one who is becoming better, no matter how bad she may be at the moment. And the bad person is one who, whatever her present state of virtue, is becoming worse. This may sound surprising, but I think there is great truth in Dewey's observation. I try to explain it to my students by asking the following question: If your goal was to reach the summit of a hill, would you rather be near the top of the hill rolling down, or near the bottom moving up? In the former case, my present situation looks good, but the future is not very promising! By contrast, the person at the bottom of the hill moving up may not be very happy about her present state. But the future is full of promise. She is moving in the right direction. What she needs now is patience and persevering hope.

Can we tell, though, whether we are in fact growing? Earlier in this chapter I suggested several reliable indicators of genuine growth, even though we may still be burdened with the sickness-sin of Romans 7. Let me just add that, in my experience, we cannot really recognize authentic growth from day to day. We need a wider perspective. That is, I can see growth in my own spiritual life if I compare my values and attitudes today with those I lived by five or ten or forty years ago. The longer the time span, the clearer the growth. When I take the long-range view (and the same is true when I look at the lives of those I direct), it is clear, for example, that my dependence on the Lord and my realization of the unimportance of human approval are much greater today than they were when I was ordained. I still confess to failings in these areas. But the frustration this engenders is greatly diminished when I reflect that there has indeed been growth over the years. Realizing that, I can continue the struggle and persevere in hope.

So we should focus on love rather than on holiness, and on growth rather than on achieved or unachieved perfection. The third focus I suggested, at the beginning of this section, is holy realism. This is actually the attitude underlying the two previous suggestions. What I mean by realism is this: we should not set impossible goals for ourselves or others. We should not live in a fantasy world of unrealistic expectations. Positively, we should know and accept our real human situation. "If wishes were horses, beggars would ride," we used to say when I was a boy. A favorite example of mine of this holy realism is Mary Magdalene. If she had spent her life lamenting the fact that she was not the innocent disciple John, Magdalene would have wasted the only life she had to live. For all eternity she is the converted prostitute. That is her history and her glory.

At the same time our realism, like Mary's, should be "holy." That is, we realize that God has accepted us as we are, and has committed himself to the work of our transformation. Magdalene is not only the ex-prostitute. Nor does her reform of life depend only on her own efforts. She is the converted prostitute. She has turned to Jesus, placed her life in his hands. Now her life-project is his, not hers. To be realistic now means accepting her history, and allowing him to work in her in his own way and at his own pace. For us, it means trusting him, that he cares for us more than we do for ourselves — and that he knows what is best for us. In other words, we believe in the common sense of God. And we show our common sense by loving in the same way that we are loved. This will be our topic in the following chapters.

Part 2

The Signs
of a
Common-Sensical
God

Chapter 3

Biblical Wisdom and Common Sense

Underlying all that we have said in Part One is the fundamental conviction that God is sensible, and that our call to be like God, to be holy, is essentially a call to be people of good sense. The problem, as I see it, is that common sense is not really very common, and that many good people do not seem to credit him with much common sense. They think of God as arbitrary, demanding, and unpredictable. Like the friends of Job, they feel that human beings can only submit or rebel in the face of the mysterious ways of the divine — and that the holy way is to submit, without understanding the how or the why.

There is, at least at first glance, some biblical basis for this attitude. Perhaps the most famous Old Testament reference cited is Isaiah 55:8-9: "For my thoughts are not your thoughts, my ways are not your ways — it is Yahweh who speaks. Yes, the heavens are as high above the earth as my ways are above your ways, my thoughts above your thoughts." But we must read this passage and the related verse, Micah 4:12, in context. The point is Yahweh's call to conversion, and the contrast is between human ideas of sin and forgiveness and Yahweh's ideas thereof. "Let the wicked man abandon his way, the evil man his thoughts.

Let him turn back to Yahweh who will take pity on him, to our God who is rich in forgiving." This is where Yahweh's thoughts and ways are far beyond our human ways. God is not vindictive, grudge-bearing, unwilling to forgive and forget. The point is not that God is arbitrary and unpredictable, but that his vision is so much broader and his heart so much more open than ours can ever be.

But what of Paul's equally famous exclamation in Romans 11:33-34? There he says, quoting Isaiah 40:13: "How rich are the depths of God — how deep his wisdom and knowledge — and how impossible to penetrate his motives or understand his methods. `Who could ever know the mind of the Lord? Who could ever be his counsellor?'" Here, too, we must consider the context. Paul has been speaking of God's call to Israel, which he sees as still valid even in the New Covenant of Jesus. God is faithful, and continues even now to work for the conversion of the chosen people, despite their rejection of the Son. Again, what is amazing to Paul is the greatness of heart of this faithful God of ours; God (once known to us) is consistent and predictable, whereas we are inconsistent. It is we who are arbitrary and unreasonable, not God.

It is in this light that we must understand the injunction of Paul in Philippians 2:5: "Let this mind be in you which was also in Christ Jesus"; and his claim in 1 Corinthians 2:16 that in fact "we are those who have the mind of Christ." In Philippians the call is to be unselfish, united in love, concerned with one another's interests rather than our own. In Corinthians Paul is speaking of the spiritual person who, inspired by the Spirit of God, judges everything in a godly way. It is clear in both passages that God's love is supremely reasonable and consistent, and that we are called to be like him. But it is also clear that the common sense of God is not merely natural wisdom. Nor is the common sense to which we are called natural to us in our sinful condition. It is an "inspirited," Spirit-filled wisdom. Our natural vision is distorted; as long as we ourselves do not see clearly, God's ways (like the parent's ways from the perspective of the small child) may well appear arbitrary and unpredictable. But the problem is not with God's ways; it is rather with our distorted vision. Paul is calling us to see with the eyes of God.

Wisdom in the Old Testament

The dictionary defines *common sense* as "ordinary good sense or sound practical judgment." As I reflected on this definition in the light of scripture, it occurred to me to consult McKenzie's *Dictionary of the Bible* again — this time his entry for *wisdom*. I recalled that wisdom was the one gift Solomon asked of Yahweh, and that his request seems to be closely-connected with good practical judgment. In his dream at Gibeon (1 Kgs 3:4-14) Solomon was told by the Lord: "Ask what you would like me to give you." And he replied, after thanking Yahweh for favoring the house of his father, David, that he found himself very young and inexperienced for the challenge of governing the many people of Israel. So he asked: "Give your servant a heart to understand how to discern between good and evil, for who could govern this people that is so great?" Yahweh was pleased with Solomon's request for a discerning heart and gladly granted it. "Here and now I do what you ask. I give you a heart wise and shrewd as none before you has had and none will have after you."

Solomon is the proverbial wise man. But, as I suspected and McKenzie confirmed, the gift of wisdom in the Bible is not restricted to Solomon or to the rulers of Israel. Indeed, the idea of wisdom was widespread in the ancient Near East, where it referred to "maxims on how to conduct oneself in speech and deportment." Taught by professional scribes, and learned only by instruction, wisdom sometimes went beyond practical guidelines for speaking and acting to include reflections, generally pessimistic, on the problems of life. Even then, the concern was practical — how to deal with trials and challenges — rather than speculative.

This was the cultural background of the biblical concern with wisdom. In Israel, too, wisdom was "a practical skill in action." The word was used, first of all, for the skill of a craftsman. Then it came to be applied to administrators, tribal chieftains, and others. Solomon's prayer for wisdom places him solidly in this tradition. But while much of biblical wisdom (for example, in Sirach and Proverbs) deals with maxims of conduct and practical solutions to the problems of life, and although it is also taught in scribal schools and learned from association with the wise (Prv 13:20), it was seen ultimately as a gift from Yahweh. "For Yahweh himself is giver of wisdom; from his mouth issue knowledge and discernment" (Prv 2:6; see also Sir 1:1 and Ex 31:3).

Also noteworthy in the biblical tradition is the fact that women are singled out for praise because of their wisdom and counsel: the woman of Tekoa (2 Sm 14:2); the woman who advised Joab at Abel of Beth-maacah (2 Sm 20:16); and Jael, in the song of Deborah and Barak (Jdg 5:29). Moreover, the wise person, unlike the fool, is always learning, always open to correction and instruction (Prv 9:8-9). The most significant biblical modification of the wisdom tradition, though, is that it is solidly grounded in faith in Yahweh, who alone is truly wise.

The divine wisdom is also practical knowledge, and creation is the greatest work of this wisdom. Thus the beginning and essential prerequisite of creaturely wisdom is the fear of the Lord (Prv 9:10, among others). Wise people do not find in their wisdom an occasion to boast, since they know that it is a gift and only a shadow of the true wisdom of God. "The peak of wisdom, therefore," McKenzie says, "is understanding the deeds of Yahweh, especially his judgments."

As we might expect, in later Old Testament writings wisdom comes to be equated with observance of the Law and practical judgment with guidelines for moral living. While this is not false, it is too narrow and legalistic to capture the real spirit of the wisdom tradition. I think we could sum up that tradition, and the paragraphs above, by saying that human wisdom is a gift of God, a participation in the divine wisdom, which enables us to live well and to discern his inspirations in our living. Thus it is that wisdom, a treasure granted by God (Jb 28), comes to be personified as a heavenly being (Prv 8:22-36), and as a woman, created by Yahweh, who gives "good advice and sound judgment" to those who love her (Prv 8:1-22).

The Teaching of Jesus

When we come to the New Testament, the most striking development is the identification of Jesus (as well as the Holy Spirit) with the wisdom of God. John makes this identification implicitly when Jesus' sayings about being the source of water, bread, and light echo the claims of Wisdom, especially in Proverbs. (See, for example, the *Jerusalem Bible* footnotes, 4a, 6j, and 8b, to John's gospel.) It is Paul, though, who makes explicit the identification of Christian wisdom with Christ nailed to the cross. "And so, while the Jews demand miracles and the Greeks look for wisdom, we preach Christ crucified . . . to those who have been called, whether Jew or Greek, a Christ who is the power and the wisdom of God" (1 Cor 2:22-24; see also 2:7-10; and Col 2:3).

Considering what we have said concerning the Old Testament idea of God's wisdom, this Pauline passage can be seen in a new and deeper light. The wisdom of God is shown in his "craftsman's skill" in creating the world and his good practical judgment in guiding creation to the end he has in view. And Jesus is God's wisdom. In Jesus, God works in the world, sustaining creation and fulfilling the divine design for human history. One of my favorite lines in scripture is John 5:17: "My Father works even until now, and so do I." (See also Jn 4:34; 9:4; 10:25, 37-38; and 14:12.) Our God is ever active, dynamic, shaping the world according to his grand design. God is the Master Craftsman, who loves work and does it to perfection. This is the wisdom Jesus shares with God and reveals to us.

Jesus also reveals to us, his friends and co-workers, how we can live well in this world. What is striking is that he often, explicitly or implicitly, praises the common sense, the good judgment, of the true disciple. His doctrine is not otherworldly, if by that we mean that it has no relation to the wisdom of this world. That is why he constantly uses parables in his teaching. A parable appeals to ordinary human experience to make a religious point. The kingdom of God is like a householder . . . a woman searching for a lost coin . . . a father with his prodigal son . . . a planter sowing seed . . . a Samaritan on a journey. Anyone who passed through life in a mystical fog could never make sense of the teaching of Jesus. And anyone who did not have the practicality to recognize the precise point of comparison in each parable would make very strange sense of that teaching. Obviously, God is not like the unscrupulous judge (Lk 18:1-8) in his injustice and selfishness. The single point of the parable is that we must be as persevering in our prayer for justice as the importunate widow was in hers. The Lord expects us to have enough good sense to realize that!

Jesus also frequently uses common-sense arguments in his discussions with the Pharisees: for example, in Matthew 12:1-8, where he answers their objections to the disciples' act of picking and eating corn on the Sabbath day; and in 12:9-14, where he responds to their question concerning healing on the Sabbath. He also appeals to the common sense of the disciples, as we see in his reaction to Martha's complaint in Luke 10:38-42; and in Luke 12:22-30, where he urges the disciples not to be unduly concerned about their daily needs.

There are two passages in particular, both in Matthew, where Jesus explicitly praises the man or woman of good sense. The first, 7:21-27, begins with the statement: "It is not those who say to me, 'Lord, Lord,' who will enter the kingdom of heaven, but the person who does the will of my Father in heaven." Then, after stating that claims to have prophesied, cast out demons, worked miracles in his name, will count for little on the Day of Judgment, he goes on to say: "Therefore everyone who listens to these words of mine and acts on them will be like a sensible man who built his house on rock. . . . But everyone who listens to these words of mine and does not act on them will be like a stupid man who built his house on sand." Eternal life belongs to the sensible, who not only hear and understand but match their actions to their words.

Similarly, at the very end of his public life (Mt 25:1-13), Jesus uses the famous parable of the wise and foolish virgins to make essentially the same point:

> Then the kingdom of heaven will be like this: Ten bridesmaids took their lamps and went to meet the bridegroom. Five of them were foolish and five were sensible: the foolish ones did take their lamps, but they brought no oil, whereas the sensible ones took flasks of oil as well as their lamps.

We all know the story. The bridegroom was late in coming, and the bridesmaids fell asleep. When the groom finally did arrive, the foolish bridesmaids had no oil. While they were out trying to buy more, the party began and the door to the wedding hall was closed to them. Again, this is a parable, which means that Jesus is making a single point by means of a good story from daily life. He is not encouraging us to be selfish, to refuse to share our "oil" with our improvident friends. The one lesson he wishes to teach us is clear from the final line of the story: "So stay awake, because you do not know the day or the hour." Be alert. Use your good sense in preparing for the coming of the kingdom of God while there is still time. Do not wait until "midnight" to get ready for the Lord's coming.

There are other passages, too, where Jesus teaches the disciples to be sensible, wise, and prudent in their earthly lives. In sending out the twelve apostles to proclaim the kingdom, he tells them: "Remember, I am sending you out like sheep among wolves; so be as cunning as serpents and yet as harmless as doves" (Mt 10:16).

He ends the parabolic discourse on the mystery of the kingdom of God by asking the people by the lake side: "Have you understood all this?" They said, "Yes." And he said to them: "Well, then, every scribe who becomes a disciple of the kingdom of heaven is like a householder, who brings out from his storeroom things both new and old" (Mt 13:51-52). Such a disciple has the good sense to learn from experience and to integrate the old with the new. As the *Jerusalem Bible* footnote to this verse says: "The Jewish teacher who becomes a disciple of Christ has at his disposal all the wealth of the Old Testament as well as the perfection of the New."

Likewise, Jesus begins the parable of the conscientious stewards, which immediately precedes and makes a similar point to that of the wise and foolish bridesmaids, by asking: "What sort of servant, then, is faithful and wise enough for the master to place him over his household, to give them their food at the proper time?" (Mt 24:45; see also Lk 16:8, where the dishonest steward is praised for his "astuteness.")

Perhaps we have cited enough passages to see clearly that good sense, prudence in thinking and acting, is central to the gospel teaching of Jesus. There is no doubt that the wisdom of the cross is "foolishness to the Greeks." Jesus is not just a wise moral teacher or a philosopher. The Word and Wisdom of God, which he is (and proclaims), definitely transcend our human wisdom. Transcendence, though, is not contradiction; the word *transcend* means literally "to climb beyond." Jesus calls us to climb beyond our natural ways of thinking and acting.

And yet, this world — and our human experience — is not a dream, to be rejected as illusory or unreal. Rather, we are called to see it from a new vantage point, in a new light. The mature Christian, like Job (42:5-6), can exclaim: "I knew you then only by hearsay; but now, having seen you with my own eyes, I retract all I have said, and in dust and ashes I repent." What does "seeing God" mean for Job? The story of his trials ends with his fortunes restored, with more prosperity, more children, more honor among his people. The new, purified vision of Job does not destroy or deny his life in the world; it enhances it. His human life is lived more deeply and more fully because he has encountered God. This is a good parable, it seems to me, for our attempt to integrate the folly of the cross with Jesus' call to be wise and prudent stewards in his kingdom.

To Begin to Live as Sensible Stewards

The importance of common sense in the lives of God's friends has preoccupied me for several years now. We seem to live in an age in which religion is used to justify fanaticism on both ends of the ideological spectrum. The tragedy of Bosnia, to cite the most glaring example today, stands as a witness to the fruits of a narrow-minded, unreasonable use of religious doctrine to justify oppression and bloodshed. Even in Palestine, where sensible men and women have made great progress in achieving peace, the fanatical fringes on both sides have made the peace truly precarious.

For that reason alone it seems essential to proclaim clearly that our God is a God of common sense. We blaspheme when we — whether Muslims or Jews or Christians — make God the guarantor of our irrational prejudices. To do so is to reduce God to the size of our own minds. But religious fanatics are not the only people who seem to deny the common sense of God. Even ordinary good persons, frequently see God as arbitrary, too demanding, too idealistic. They often fail to see the link between the realities of their lives and the "demands" of God. In the chapters to follow, I hope we can speak to many of their specific concerns. I would also hope, though, that these first three chapters have made clear the scriptural basis for speaking of our God as a God of common sense. For us Christians, the teaching of Jesus, with its grounding in the Old Testament, must be the ultimate source of whatever we say about God and his ways with us.

For twenty-five years now I have been involved in the formation of seminarians for the diocesan priesthood. For about seventeen of those years I have also taught a course on discernment. One of the topics we treat in the course is the discernment of religious vocations. How does a candidate determine that he or she has a vocation, a call from God, to the priestly or religious life? How does the religious congregation or seminary verify this call?

The sense of being called is an interior experience in the heart of the prospective candidate. And yet, as we saw in Chapter 2 concerning holiness in general, the inner call must show itself in visible fruits. Common sense demands that we (and the candidate) look for tangible signs of the grace of vocation. Only in that way can we be like the sensible man of whom Jesus said:

> And indeed, which of you here, intending to build a tower, would not first sit down and work out the cost, to see if he had enough to complete it? Otherwise, if he laid the foundation and then found himself unable to finish the work, the onlookers would all start making fun of him and saying, "Here is a man who started to build and was unable to finish" (Lk 14:28-30).

St. Thomas Aquinas said that grace builds on nature. God normally works through natural causes. Miracles are possible, but, by definition, they should be the rare exception and not the norm. When applied to the question of religious vocation, this means that there are certain natural qualities of personality or temperament that we should look for in assessing candidates. Raymond Hostie, in his very useful book *Discernment of Vocations* (Sheed and Ward, 1963), enumerated four such qualities which are still valid: good mental health, sufficient intelligence, lucid intellect, and a virtuous will. While "lucid intellect," as we shall see, refers specifically to good practical judgment or sound common sense, the other three also require good sense in their application.

Mental health, as I like to describe it, means that our neuroses are manageable. Bernard Basset, S.J., once wrote a popular book called *We Neurotics* (Academy Guild Press, 1962). As the title suggests, he would say (and I would agree) that all of us have our own irrational anxieties and insecurities, our neuroses. No one, at least in my experience, is fully integrated and perfectly balanced. Even the saints have their quirks of temperament. But "sound mental health" means that we can manage our neuroses, that we can function effectively and live happily despite them. My favorite example of a manageable neurosis is my own sister's irrational fear of escalators. She cannot explain it; she knows that it is irrational. But I would never recommend that she get expensive professional help to resolve her anxiety. And I would say that she has good mental health. Why? Because she has been able to live quite happily and fruitfully with her neurosis. After all, every building that has an escalator also has an elevator and a stairway.

Similarly, "sufficient intelligence" means sufficient for the work or the life-choice we have in mind. Candidates for the seminary or the convent do not need to be geniuses. But they do need to be able to handle, with reasonable ease (without harming their health or warping their personalities), the studies required to equip them for the work they will do for the kingdom of God. Even the Dominicans and the Jesuits, known for their academic apostolates, are not all meant to be PhDs. If every Jesuit were a genius, we might have a terrible time getting three meals on the table every day! But each of us does need to be well-formed to contribute fruitfully to the corporate ministry of our congregation in the church.

Hostie's terms "lucid intellect" and "virtuous will" may sound very demanding and exalted. What he means by them, however, is quite down-to-earth. A lucid intellect is one that can make good practical judgments. It is precisely the common sense of which we speak in this book. And a virtuous will is one that can act upon the common-sense judgments made. A seminarian may see clearly that he needs to be a man of prayer, and that the eucharist should be central to his priestly life. If so, his practical judgment (his "lucid intellect") is clear and solid. But if he cannot get out of bed in time for prayer and Mass — or cannot get to bed on time the evening before — the problem is with his willpower. When this happens just occasionally, we may well conclude that it is simply the "sickness" problem of Romans 7. But if resolving and failing is the daily pattern of his life, then he is lacking in the "virtuous will," the strength of will essential for a vocation in ministry.

Suppose, though, that our seminarian cannot even see the connection between priesthood and eucharist, or between getting to bed on time and praying well the next morning. In that case his problem concerns Hostie's lucid intellect. He is apparently incapable of making practical, common-sense judgments about what is necessary to live well as God's minister. While all four of Hostie's natural prerequisites are obviously important for the priestly or religious life, I believe I would give greatest importance to this one: the capacity to make sound practical judgments.

The person of good sense will be able to accept and work realistically within his or her limited intellectual capacity. If a woman knows she has an IQ of 95 (slightly below average), she will not be frustrated with average grades. She will be happy with a C+ or a B and will not be continually pushing herself beyond her limits to earn an A. Similarly, she will be able to accept and to live with her manageable neuroses. She will have enough good sense to work to strengthen her will by mortification and self-discipline, while accepting the Romans 7 side of her personality in areas where she finds herself weak.

To return to our seminarian, he may realize that he was spoiled at home and thus lacks the self-discipline to be faithful to seminary schedules. This is fine, provided he now can see the need for self-discipline and can begin to develop this quality in himself. After all, priestly or religious formation lasts several years precisely in order to give time for personal growth. What is important is that he be a mature and disciplined man by the time his bishop ordains him.

There is another, equally weighty reason why I would give greatest importance to the priest-to-be's sound common sense. And in these days of shared ministry, when religious women are seen more and more as full partners in the mission of the church, this reason would apply with equal force to them. The priest and the sister in ministry hold people's lives in their hands. What do people expect of them? Sound doctrine, of course, but also good emotional balance. The priest who cannot handle his own neuroses is going to be useless at best, and dangerous at worst, in dealing with the insecurities of his people. But the pastoral minister is, above all, a confessor, a confidant, a spiritual director. This is the very essence of the mission entrusted by Jesus to the apostles and to us. It is most essential, therefore, that we be able to help people to see the faith-meaning of their experience and decide how to respond and act. We can do great harm if we cannot bring common sense to bear on the problems they share with us.

A personal example may help here. My grandmother died almost fifty years ago, before I entered the Jesuits. In her last years she suffered from a serious heart condition. As a result, her doctor advised her to avoid crowded and enclosed places. In particular, he (a good Catholic) said she should not attend the crowded Sunday Masses at her church. Being a devout person, Grandma felt she could not follow this advice without first consulting her parish priest. He was an elderly man and, by all accounts, a good pastor. But when she approached him in the confessional and told him what her doctor had said about not attending Sunday Mass, he asked her why. "Because," she said, "the doctor told me I might die of heart failure in the crowded church." And what did he reply? "Can you think of any better place to die?"

The pastor may have been overtired, or half asleep, but we would have to say honestly that his advice was lacking in good common sense. The result was that Grandma, being a pious person, felt she had to attend Sunday Mass, whatever the risk, "because Father said so." Even my own father was upset when Grandma told him. As I said earlier, my dad took out his handkerchief whenever the Pope sneezed. But he was also a man of great good sense, and he could see that the advice she received from the pastor was not sensible. Unfortunately, he could not convince her. Happily, Grandma did not die during Sunday Mass. At least Dad's faith was not put to that ultimate test.

We have been speaking of the importance in the ministry of sound common sense. It is necessary to stress, however, that good sense (as well as the other qualities we have discussed) is important for any Christian vocation. In my course I discuss these qualities in speaking of discerning religious vocations. But one of the practicum questions I ask the students to reflect upon is this: Should these qualities also be required, and verified, in the case of couples preparing for marriage? The class is a good mix of seminarians and religious as well as lay persons, single and married. What is striking is that it is the married students who answer "Yes!" most emphatically. Having committed themselves to the vocation of marriage, and having faced its challenges for several years, they are convinced that married couples need as good and as solid a preparation as do priests and religious.

I think their views, and the forcefulness with which they express them, make quite an impression on the seminarians and the sisters present. They begin to realize, as perhaps they had not before, that every Christian vocation is a challenge — and that the good sense Jesus inculcates in so many of his sermons and parables is essential to every Christian vocation. That, I believe, is what my mother was trying to tell me when she said that "even the best of marriages requires a great deal of dying to self on the part of both spouses." Hopefully, the seminarians and religious can learn early the lesson of holy realism. If so, they will have a new vision of, and a deeper respect for, the marital vocations of their parents and their friends. Then, perhaps, they (and the church) can do a better job of preparing couples to live well the great vocation of marriage.

Chapter 4

Contemplation and Common Sense

We have spoken much of common sense and its importance in the Bible and in Christian life today. One crucial aspect of our discussion is that wisdom, good practical judgment, is seen as God's gift to the people of God. This is evident in the New Testament as well as in the Old. As St. Paul says:

> The hidden wisdom of God which we teach in our mysteries is the wisdom that God predestined to be for our glory before the world began. It is a wisdom that none of the masters of this age have ever known, or they would never have crucified the Lord of glory; we teach what scripture calls "the things that no eye has seen and no ear has heard, things beyond the human mind, all that God has prepared for those who love him" (1 Cor 2:7-9).

When I began to think about writing this book, my conviction was that, since our God is a God of common sense, those who are growing in holiness should become more and more like him, and their experience of the Lord should make them wiser, more sensible persons. The challenge for me in writing, then, was to flesh out, to substantiate that conviction. It seems clear from all that we have said that common sense, wisdom, is an essential element in the discipleship to which Jesus calls us and, at the same time, the fruit of God's work in us. St. Paul explicitly makes the latter point when he goes on to say:

> These are the very things that God has revealed to us through the Spirit, for the Spirit reaches the depths of everything, even the depths of God. . . . Now instead of the spirit of the world, we have received the Spirit that comes from God, to teach us to understand the gifts that he has given us" (1 Cor 2:10,12).

It is clear, then, that the common sense of which we speak is not merely a natural virtue, which some people possess and others do not. Grace, it is true, does build on nature: natural good sense can be a valuable foundation for acquiring the mind of Christ. But such wisdom goes beyond any natural quality we may possess. It is a gift of God. The question, then, is this: How do we acquire this gift? By what means does God give us the Spirit? We know that the Spirit is given initially in baptism, and in a more mature way in confirmation (and the other sacraments). But these, I believe, are just the peak moments in a lifelong, ongoing process of transformation. It is to that process that we refer in speaking of contemplation in relation to common sense.

The Meaning of Contemplation

One of the problems we encounter in seeking help from the great figures in the history of Christian spirituality is that the word *contemplation* has had different meanings in different traditions. On my own journey, the Carmelite and the Jesuit traditions have been most influential. Both are what we might call spiritualities of the heart. That is, they focus more on the will and on love than on the intellect and understanding. In this they differ (in emphasis, at least) from the more intellectually-oriented tradition of St. Thomas Aquinas and the Dominicans. For Thomas, contemplation is the graced act of knowing God, culminating in heaven in the beatific vision. Thomas, of course, would not deny the importance of love — as is clear from his great eucharistic hymns, like the *Pange Lingua* ("Sing, my tongue, the Savior's glory") for the feast of Corpus Christi. It is a question, rather, of emphasis.

While Thomas has been a very great, probably the greatest, influence in my philosophical and theological formation, St. John of the Cross and St. Teresa of Avila, the Carmelite masters, as well as St. Ignatius, the founder of my own Jesuit community, have most influenced my spiritual formation. I suspect, moreover, that these mystics have had a similar influence on most serious pray-ers today. Even within these traditions of the heart, however, the word *contemplation* has had two different meanings. For Ignatius, it refers to one of the two methods he proposes to receptive beginners in the interior life. For Teresa and John, by contrast, it refers to a more mature stage in the life of prayer. Since I speak of contemplation from within these two affective traditions, let us explain more fully the meaning of contemplation for each of them.

St. Ignatius Loyola developed the *Spiritual Exercises* as a tool (the first retreat in the church, it seems) to bring beginners to a life of total, committed service of Jesus Christ and his church. He had in mind people like Francis Xavier, men and women who were good, devout Christians (perhaps like the rich young man of Mark 10:17-22), but not very clear or deep in their commitment. The Exercises were a means to win them to a wholehearted dedication to Jesus and his cause.

Ignatius proposed to these beginners two principal methods of prayer: meditation and contemplation. To summarize briefly, meditation involves using the understanding, the reasoning, to come to know the Lord in scripture, and to grasp the meaning of his gospel message for us. Contemplation, on the other hand, is the use of the imagination to attain the same end. It involves being part of the event we are contemplating, being there imaginatively, seeing and hearing, and even tasting and touching and smelling. Contemplation is like a good movie, in that we enter into the drama ourselves; meditation is thinking about the event and its application to our lives. Clearly the two are not mutually exclusive. I have met people who "have no imagination," and so find contemplation difficult if not impossible. And I have known others who are highly imaginative, and yet they find the more analytical activity of meditating very difficult. Most of us, however, can do both, and our prayer as beginners is probably a blend of the two.

Whatever our temperament, it is important to keep in mind that meditation and contemplation are both but means to an end. The end is to come to know the Jesus of the gospels and to discover his call to us: who he is for us, and what he calls us to do or to be. It is not important which means we use (a beginner usually has to experiment with both and discover which is most helpful) as long as the end is achieved.

So, since our concern here is with Ignatian contemplation, we can summarize by saying that for Ignatius, contemplation is a beginner's technique for coming to know Jesus Christ as the Lord of our lives. It involves using the imagination to enter into, and to become part of, the gospel scene we are contemplating. Its success is measured not by the detail and vividness of our imaginative exercise, but by the degree to which it enlightens our minds and thereby moves our wills. Ignatius' ultimate goal is not a beautiful prayer experience but a real, solid commitment to Jesus and his kingdom.

Teresa of Avila and John of the Cross are quite aware of Ignatian contemplation. It is, after all, a part of the long tradition which they, as fellow Spaniards and younger contemporaries of Ignatius, also shared. But they do not call it contemplation. They refer instead to "meditating with the understanding or with the imagination." Teresa especially, who writes much more for beginners than John does, gives numerous examples of what Ignatius would call contemplation — especially in her famous discussion of the Our Father in *The Way of Perfection*, which she wrote to teach her own sisters mental prayer. John, who was twenty-seven years younger than Teresa (and about fifty years younger than Ignatius), is undoubtedly thinking of that book when he says that he does not write for beginners, precisely because others have already done so quite adequately.

John and Teresa do, however, speak of contemplation. In fact, the word is central to their teaching and to the Carmelite tradition. What they mean by it, though, is quite different from Ignatian imaginative meditation. For both Teresa and John, contemplation is the more mature stage of prayer in which God does more and more and the pray-er does less and less. They do not mean by this a prayer of visions and ecstasies and revelations. While Teresa spends more time than John (especially in the last three "Mansions" of her *Interior Castle*) discussing such preternatural phenomena, and seems to see more value in them, she is quite clear that they are not essential to holiness.

It is John, her spiritual director for many years, who distinguishes most sharply between contemplation and such preternatural experiences as ecstasy. For him, the latter have virtually nothing to do with holiness and should generally be ignored by the pray-er. His reason, expressed most clearly in Books Two and Three of *The Ascent of Mount Carmel*, is that such experiences are very difficult to evaluate. The devil can produce all of them. (I am always reminded here of the competition between Moses and the magicians of Egypt in

Exodus, Chapter 7.) They can also be the product of a strong imaginative temperament. In any case, even if they are genuine, John tells us it is best not to pay much attention to them. They are not essential to holiness, and they can distract us from the important work of God in us.

What, then, is contemplation for John and Teresa? As I said above, it is a more mature stage of the life of prayer. In the beginning, for example in Ignatian contemplation, we are quite active in our prayer. God is the primary agent, of course, but works through our natural faculties and with our active cooperation. Gradually, though, we find ourselves less inclined, and indeed less able, to do much at prayer. Teresa calls these beginnings of contemplation (in the Carmelite sense) "the prayer of quiet." We become "patients" rather than agents when we pray. Both Teresa and John see this growing passivity as the normal experience of any faithful pray-er. It is not something extraordinary or "very high." From a natural point of view, of course, it is extraordinary. But then, so is the entire Spirit-life, which Paul sees as the new way of being of every baptized Christian. Once we enter into this new life by baptism, however, and once we make an adult commitment to live that life seriously, Teresa and John's contemplation is the normal goal (on this earth) of the process into which we have entered.

This contemplation, though, is itself a process. (I tried to describe the process in chapters three to five of *When the Well Runs Dry*, and in Part 1 of *Drinking from a Dry Well*.) A joyful quiet and easy passivity gradually gives way to the darker, more empty experience John calls "the dark night."

He says explicitly that this dark night *is* contemplation. The dry well, the cloud of unknowing, the prayer of faith (Leonard Boase's phrase), the dark night — all of these are metaphorical names for the experience of mature contemplation. As all of them imply, it is far from

being an ecstatic, visionary experience. It is, rather, an experience of transformation; and the best analogy I can find to describe it is the person on the operating table undergoing surgery.

When a person has major surgery, the doctor anesthetizes the patient during the operation. I come from a family of doctors on my mother's side, and we believed as children that anesthesia was to prevent pain. Now I think I know better. The doctor puts the patient to sleep primarily to prevent the person from interfering with the operation. A conscious patient would be tense, anxious, perhaps trying to prevent the incision or to help the doctor. Or, if the patient were like me, there would be continual questions about what the doctor was doing. (That is why my father found it difficult to teach me plumbing or carpentry or any other skill. I had too many questions, and he could not attend to the job he was doing!) So the doctor gives the patient anesthesia in order to get on with the business of saving a life.

The dark night is like that. We don't know what the Lord is doing — precisely so that he can get on, unimpeded, with his work of healing and transformation. But we can carry our analogy further. Suppose we visit a friend after surgery, and we ask her how the operation went. And suppose she replies: "Ah! It was a failure. I will have to undergo the whole procedure again." When we ask why she responds: "Because I was unconscious the entire time. I don't remember a thing that happened." What would we say to her? I know what I would say: "For heaven's sake, take a look at your side (assuming she had an appendectomy) and see if you have an incision you did not have before! See if your nausea and your pain are gone." In other words, we judge the operation not by the experience the patient had on the table, but by the difference it now makes in her life.

The analogy to the prayer of the dark night is perhaps clear. What is important now is not our experience during the time of prayer, but the way the prayer transforms our attitudes and values. If we find ourselves more generous, more patient, more sensitive to the needs of others, more desirous of living totally for God, then our prayer is fruitful and good — even if it is filled with distractions and seems, humanly speaking, a waste of time. Once mature pray-ers realize this, they can be at peace in the dryness and darkness. They don't enjoy it, of course, any more than any normal person enjoys major surgery. But they can value what they do not enjoy, precisely because they have some sense of the transforming work God is accomplishing in the dry darkness.

As I see it, we can compare the stages of a good prayer relationship to the stages of human love: courtship, honeymoon, and midlife. In courtship the focus is on knowing the other person and ourselves. When we speak of prayer, the other person is Jesus Christ, God, whom we come to know by meditating upon and contemplating (in the Ignatian sense) the gospels. On the honeymoon the focus shifts from knowing to loving; our prayer is more a joyful presence to the Lord we love, rather than the earlier period of discovery. (This is William Connolly's sense of contemplation, which we discussed in Chapter 2.) But the honeymoon does not last forever. We move, gradually but inexorably, into what I have somewhat loosely called midlife, since this phase lasts, even as in a good marriage, for the rest of our natural lives. It is the move from loving to truly loving. We move from loving because of what we get from the relationship to loving the other person for his or her (or, in prayer, God's) own sake. It is the precise fruit of what John of the Cross and Teresa of Avila call contemplation.

God Meeting Us Where We Are

This fruit of contemplation, in Teresa and John's sense, is transformation. We no longer go to prayer, as in the courtship period, primarily for knowledge of God and our-selves, or even primarily to experience the Lord, as during the honeymoon of our prayer lives. What God is doing in the dark night is effecting our transformation, so that one day we may be able to love as we are loved. Of course, this has been his goal from the very beginning; as we come to understand and accept the dry well, though, it becomes our goal too. Then we can be at home in the dryness or darkness, not because we enjoy it but because we can see its value, the change it effects in us.

It is primarily this Carmelite sense of contemplation that I had in mind in saying that contemplation should make us wiser, more common-sensical. The Lord's dark work of transformation should make us more like him; and this means, I believe, that we should become wise in the way he is wise. We should be more shaped to his hand (to use an Ignatian phrase), more able to look at the world through his eyes and to respond to it as he does. But since, as we said a moment ago, this work of transformation is God's goal from the very beginning of our prayer lives, we should be able to see wisdom, good practical judgment, as one of the major fruits of all three of the stages we have described. Anyone whose prayer is genuine should, from the very beginning, be acquiring the common sense of God.

St. John the Evangelist can help us to see this. Characteristically, when he recounts the call of the first dis-ciples (Jn 1:35-51), he does not give us a list of the twelve apostles, as the other evangelists do. He presupposes the facts which the others (whose gospels were written fifteen to thirty years earlier) recount. John's concern, typically, is with the meaning of their call. He gives us a theology of vocation, which includes three points: God always makes the first move, either directly or through another human being; God takes each of us (and each apostle) precisely where we are, in our uniqueness; and finally, God's call is never compelling. God respects our freedom — inviting us and awaiting our response.

God always makes the first move. As Jesus says in the Last Supper discourse: "You did not choose me; no, I chose you, and I commissioned you to go out and bear fruit, fruit that will last" (Jn 15:16). We see this clearly in John's account of the call of the first disciples. There are five: Andrew and John himself, then Peter, Philip, and finally Nathanael. In each case it is Jesus who makes the first move. He calls Philip directly, but usually he works through a human instrument. John the Baptist points out the Lamb of God to Andrew and John. Andrew, in turn, calls his brother Peter. And Philip calls Nathanael. In our lives, too, God normally works through the instrumentality — the preaching or good example — of another human being. There are "Philips" even today, who come to Christ through a direct, interior experience of him. But most of us, like most of the disciples, are helped by the "John the Baptists" in our lives.

The second element of John's theology of vocation is that God approaches each of us where we are, in a highly personal way. John and Andrew, we could say, are the poets, the sensitive souls. Their encounter with the Lord has a mysterious, almost mystical quality about it. "What do you want?" "Rabbi, where do you live?" "Come and see." And they did go, and they saw, and they stayed with him. John even tells us, "It was about the tenth hour (4 p.m.)." Why does he mention the time of day? Because that was the moment when John fell in love, when his whole life was transformed by his meeting with Jesus.

Peter's initial encounter with the Lord is quite different, because Peter is a very different person — dramatic and impulsive. The very first thing Jesus does is to change his name: "You are Simon, son of John; you are to be called Cephas (Peter), meaning 'Rock.'" The more cautious, reflective John and Andrew would probably have been frightened away by such a dramatically direct approach, but it suits Peter's personality perfectly.

The contrast is even more striking if we compare Peter's call with Philip's or Nathanael's. Philip is the simple, unimaginative one. At the Last Supper he interrupts Jesus' talk about being one with the Father, which is too deep and confusing for him, by appealing to Jesus: "Lord, just let us see the Father, and then we shall be satisfied" (Jn 14:8). So, how does Jesus call Philip in John 1:43? He simply calls him: no mystical depths, and no dramatic change of name — which Peter loved, but Philip would have found totally confusing. After all, he was called Philip on his driver's license and his baptismal certificate. And all his family called him Philip. How could Jesus change his name now? So Jesus takes Philip where he is and says, very simply: "Follow me."

Finally, Nathanael is the good Pharisee, the man of the law. Jesus also meets him where he is, discussing with him how any good can come from Nazareth. He explains the messianic hopes of the Law and the Prophets to Nathanael, the lover of the Law.

Not only does Jesus meet each of us where we are in our uniqueness, but he also respects our freedom totally. John and Andrew had to decide to "come and see." So did Peter and Philip and Nathanael. The decision to do so was not as immediate and wholehearted as John's account might lead us to think. One of the central themes of Mark's gospel is the first disciples' slowness to comprehend and their hesitancy to respond totally. Jesus was infinitely patient with them, sometimes to the point of exasperation (Mk 7:18; 8:17, 33; 9:18-19). He respected their freedom and their unfreedom. He danced to their music, while teaching them to dance to his.

I said at the beginning of this section that John's account of the disciples' call could help us to see that any sincere pray-er, from the outset of the life of prayer, should be acquiring the common sense of God. As John reflected on his first encounter with the Lord, and as he relived it in his imagination, he came to see the real meaning of the events at Bethany beside the Jordan River. Contemplation, in Ignatius' sense, enabled him to see his life through the eyes of God. Moreover, he invites all of us, who did not know the Lord in the flesh but who would be drawn to him in the centuries to follow, to learn from his experience — to learn who the Lord is for us and to what he is calling us. "These (signs) are recorded so that you may believe that Jesus is the Christ, the Son of God, and that believing you may have life through his name" (Jn 20:31). Through our imaginative contemplation of the gospels, we begin to see the wisdom of God at work in our own lives.

As our life of discipleship moves on, Jesus gradually becomes personally real to us (Connolly's sense of contemplation). Not only do we think about, and find ourselves touched by, the apostles' encounter with him, but now we begin to write our own "fifth gospel," the story of our own heart-to-heart encounter with our Savior. This is the honeymoon stage of our life of prayer, when the Lord begins to shape our hearts to the pattern of his own heart — now directly, and no longer (or not so much) through the "John the Baptists" in our lives. I find a beautiful echo of this transition in chapter 4 of John's gospel. The Samaritan woman, after her encounter with Jesus at the well, "hurried back to the town to tell the people, 'Come and see a man who told me everything I ever did; I wonder if he is the Christ.' This brought people out of the town and they started walking towards him" (4:28-30). She is their "John the Baptist": many came to believe in Jesus because she told them about him and brought them to him. And yet, at the end of the incident they say to her: "Now we no longer believe because of what you told us; we have heard him ourselves and we know that he really is the Savior of the world" (4:42). Their own honeymoon with the Lord, when he can work directly and personally in their lives, has begun.

Meeting God Where He Is

It was not really clear to the Samaritans, of course, what this first encounter with the Lord meant. Nor was it clear to the apostles, even after Peter proclaimed Jesus to be "the Christ, the Son of the living God" (Mt 16:16). That is the way with honeymoons. We think we have found perfection, and our only concern is to make it last forever. But the truth is that we are just beginning to know the Lord, to have the mind of Christ. It is a very good beginning, but we still have a long way to journey. At the end of our lives we will surely value midlife, with all of its crises, much more than the honeymoon. At least we will if our experience has brought us any closer to the common sense of God.

Peter receives his first shock immediately after his profession of faith in Jesus. In a few verses he goes from heaven to hell. First, Jesus blesses him for his discerning judgment: "Simon, son of Jonah, you are a happy man! Because it was not flesh and blood that revealed this to you but my Father in heaven." But then Jesus goes on to reveal to them his own destiny as Messiah: to go to Jerusalem, to suffer and die, and to be raised up on the third day. Peter is scandalized. As a good Jew, he is convinced that the Messiah, the Christ, will be a triumphant political leader. He cannot imagine that the messianic victory will involve suffering, humiliation, and death. So he remonstrates with Jesus: "Lord, this must not happen to you." And now Jesus, who had just blessed him as God-inspired, says to poor Peter: "Get behind me, Satan! You are an obstacle in my path, because the way you think is not God's way but man's."

Peter must have been crushed, since he really did love the Lord. As the years passed, however, he also must have realized that he spoke for every man and woman who would ever follow Jesus. None of us, when we begin to love the Lord, knows what this loves means or entails. We find that our common sense our natural way of judging and perceiving — is very far from, and can even be an obstacle to, the wisdom of God, which is Christ crucified. In our honeymoon days we love according to our own lights — according to our own idea of love. We are sincere, but we do not know this mysterious God of ours, or ourselves, as well as we think.

That is why, if we persevere in prayer (as in marriage), we come to value midlife more than the honeymoon. We begin to realize that what is most valuable is not necessarily most enjoyable. We learn what it means to love "for better or worse." That, of course, is the common sense of God. But only God can make it ours — by means of the surgery of the dark night or the dry well. In fact, I would see this as the very heart of the transformation process which takes place in the dark night. To see and love reality — God and the world and ourselves — as God sees and loves: this is the real work accomplished in the long years of the dry well. To the extent that the Lord has been able to accomplish it in us, we will judge persons and situations as he does. We will share his practical judgment, his common sense.

Thus we have seen that contemplation, in its different meanings at various stages of our life of prayer, helps us to acquire the mind of Christ. It is, in fact, the primary means which God uses to shape us, to share with us the divine common sense. In the chapters to follow, I would like to discuss some concrete fruits of this transformation — some of the ways in which the mature friend of God comes to look at the world with divine common sense.

Let me end this chapter, though, by sharing a puzzle from my own reflection on life. Elizabeth Taylor, the famous actress, and I are almost exactly the same age. She was born in 1932, about three weeks before I was. She was the first love of my life when she appeared in the movie "National Velvet." Thus it has puzzled me, as the years passed, that she came to have eight husbands while I did not manage a single wife. (One friend, when I told this story, said that it was because she is so much better-looking than I am!) Why has she married eight times? I don't believe it is because she is a "bad person"; she has given herself to several noble and charitable causes. I suspect the problem is that each time she married she expected the honeymoon to last forever. When it did not, as it could not, she seems to have felt that the reason was because she chose the wrong partner. And so she tried again with another.

I can only guess at Elizabeth Taylor's thinking. But the pattern I have described is certainly one I have encountered often enough, both with married persons and with pray-ers. They don't seem to realize that love, divine or human, is not, and should not be, one long honeymoon. Midlife is difficult, but it is the only road to growth. For the pray-er, this means that the dry well or dark night is not, as natural common sense would see it, a sign of failure or disaster. It is, rather, the time to bring to perfection the good work God has begun in us. Perhaps coming to realize that is one of the best signs that we are acquiring the common sense of God.

Part Three

The Common Sense of the Friend of God

Chapter 5

A Sensible Life of Prayer

Every year at San Jose Seminary, ten to fifteen men are ordained as diocesan priests. Since San Jose is a national seminary, with our seminarians coming from about forty dioceses all over the Philippines, the ordinations are held at different times (usually between March and June) and in many different places. As a result, it is not possible for all of the faculty to be present at every ordination. Often enough, I find myself writing a letter of congratulation to a new priest-to-be. The thought that most frequently comes to my mind is this: I hope he will be as happy in his ministry as I have been in mine. That, as I tell him, is really the best prayer I can offer for him. Priesthood, like every life lived wholeheartedly, is difficult and challenging. There are always ups and downs, sunny days and dark days. But, as I look back on thirty-one years of ministry, I cannot imagine having been happier in any other vocation.

What makes the priestly ministry so satisfying? For me, surprisingly perhaps, the most fulfilling part of my life as a priest has been my work as a confessor and a spiritual director. The eucharist, of course, is the heart of my priestly and Christian life. In celebrating the Mass, though, I encounter people en masse. I meet them as a worshipping community. In the confessional and in spiritual direction, I meet them at a deeper and more personal level of their being. It is there that real people come fully alive for me. I learn much more about what it means to be human, and I discover the endlessly varied ways in which the Lord works with those he loves.

It is also in confession and direction that I come to realize how much alike we human beings are, despite our individuality. Oftentimes, for example, people begin their confession very hesitantly, saying, "Father, I hope I don't shock you with what I am about to confess." I am always tempted to tell them: "If you can surprise me, I will give you a free trip to Hong Kong!" Very rarely do I hear anything new in confession. The patterns of human sinfulness seem to be quite well-defined and common. Sad and sometimes sordid, yes, but almost never new. This realization helps me to follow the advice of a wise moral theology professor of many years ago. No matter what we hear in the confessional, he told us, we have no right to become angry with the penitents. Whatever they may have done, they have not offended us, the confessors. If the Lord wishes to become angry, fine, but we have no business doing so.

That is the kind of divine good sense that we learn by experience — as well as from wise teachers and elders — and which we wish to discuss in this and the following chapter. It is the fruit of a reflective, contemplative digesting of our experience of the ways of the Lord. Here is another example of how this common sense has been a fruit of my pastoral experience: Occasionally devout souls, usually novices in the life of deeper prayer, will say to me: "Father, I am the greatest of sinners." They are quite sincere, but I still feel it is my responsibility to puncture their balloon. "Why do you have to be outstanding?" I ask them. "What makes you feel you excel as a sinner? After all, the

Lord has known Genghis Khan and Hitler and Stalin. Do you really think you are a greater sinner than they?"

I do not mean to be unkind. But the fact of the matter is that most of us are not really outstanding, even in our sinning. We don't even do that very well! Our real sin is our mediocrity, our lukewarmness, our drab ordinariness. That is why I don't have to make good on my (imagined) offer of a free trip to Hong Kong! I know that St. Teresa of Avila called herself the greatest of sinners. And there is a sense in which she was speaking truly. I think she meant that, considering the ways in which the Lord had blessed her, she could not imagine anyone else — even Genghis Khan — responding as little as she had. If that was indeed her point, she is not really comparing herself to other sinners; rather, she is comparing her personal response with God's loving initiative in her own life. From that point of view, her words express a profound truth, one that each of us could proclaim.

If I had had the privilege, however, of being St. Teresa's spiritual director, I would have made the same response as I have given to others. That is, I would want to help her to make sure that her piety and spirituality were grounded in good, healthy common sense. The fact of the matter is that Teresa was not the greatest of sinners. And true holiness cannot be based on pious exaggeration, however well-meaning; it must always be grounded on truth. The common sense of Jesus in the gospels demands as much. "If you make my word your home, you will indeed be my disciples; you will learn the truth, and the truth will make you free" (Jn 8:31-32).

The "Principle and Foundation" of Sound Spirituality

In the earlier chapters we laid a good foundation for seeing common sense as a key quality of any mature spirituality. Scripture has revealed to us a God of practical

judgment, who created and guides the world wisely. We
have also seen Jesus' praise of the sensible steward, who
uses his gifts of nature and grace to cooperate in the
growth of the kingdom of God. Then we reviewed the
pattern of a good prayer life, the stages of contemplation
whereby, as the masters of our spiritual tradition tell us,
the Lord shapes us into such sensible stewards.

This wise stewardship, as we shall see, reveals itself in
many concrete details and situations in our lives. There is,
however, a basic attitude, a fundamental orientation, which
grounds all these specific details. St. Ignatius Loyola refers
to it as the "principle and foundation" of our whole life in
God. He presents it at the very beginning of his *Spiritual
Exercises:*

> We were created to praise, reverence and serve God our
> Lord, and by this means to save our souls. The other
> things on the face of the earth were created for our sake,
> and in order to help us in achieving the end for which we
> were created. Consequently, we ought to make use of
> them only insofar as they help us to attain our end, and
> withdraw from them insofar as they hinder us (#23).

Ignatius is affirming, as do all the saints, that our only
end in life is the glory of God and our own salvation.
Everything else — life, honor, work, friendship, everything
— is for us but a means to this single end. Therefore, as he
goes on to say, "we should make ourselves indifferent to all
created things, in all that is left to the liberty of our free will
and is not forbidden . . . desiring and choosing only that
which leads us more directly to the end for which we were
created." This is a very lofty ideal; to a beginner it can seem
almost inhuman. I know it struck me that way when I was
making my first Ignatian retreat as a novice in 1949. Over
the years, though, I have come to understand better what
Ignatius means — and how true it is.

In the first place, Ignatius is not saying that creatures are evil. John of the Cross helps us here. He says that all creation is good, and that no created reality is in itself an obstacle to loving God. The problem is not with creatures, but with our disordered desires (our "inordinate attachments," as Ignatius calls them in the first paragraph of the *Spiritual Exercises*) with regard to them. The problem arises when our love of creatures competes with our love for God.

Second, in calling creatures "means," Ignatius is not suggesting (as it might appear to us today), that we should use other people for our own personal ends. Other persons also belong to God, and Ignatius would be the last to suggest that we should manipulate them, use them, simply as instruments for our own benefit. No one likes the "fair weather friend," who knows us and is friendly with us only in the hope of gaining something from the friendship.

Related to the difficulty with the word *means* is Ignatius' proposal that we should "make ourselves indifferent to all created things." In the total context of the *Spiritual Exercises*, indifferent cannot mean "uncaring, cold, lacking in human affection." Ignatius was a man who loved intensely and was greatly loved by others. But he was single-minded in the sense that all of his human loves were subordinate to his centering, overmastering love of the Lord. The indifference he proposes is an attempt to right the balance when our attachment to creatures is disordered or excessive. As I like to express it, with my philosophy of science background, we can have many planetary loves in our solar system, but we can have only one sun, one centering love for God. I used this image in Chapter 1, when insisting that human love is good and necessary for true holiness. The planets are fine — as long as they don't compete with the sun for the central place in our hearts.

The problem, of course, is that they do in fact compete.

My love for my family and friends made it difficult for me to follow the Lord's call to religious life. My love for my native land and culture was a problem when I embarked on a missionary vocation. And now, my attachment to life and health and apostolic effectiveness makes for some uneasy moments as I face the inevitability of old age and death. The difference at present is that I have come to understand and appreciate what St. Ignatius meant. All of these attachments are quite normal for any human being. They can even be good, if awareness of them leads me to surrender them to the Lord, to renew my conviction that God alone is my portion and my hope, to realize how great his love must be if all these other beautiful loves are but a shadow of God's beauty. This is what Ignatian "indifference" means to me now. Far from being inhuman, it seems the only way to be truly human.

There is one phrase of Ignatius to which I would have to take exception — or, at least, express more clearly. Ignatius says "we should make ourselves indifferent" to all except God. To the extent that I have grown in Ignatian indifference, it has not been my own project. I have not made myself indifferent; it is the love of God at work in me that has effected a change in my attitudes and values. I feel, moreover, that I still have a long way to go in becoming truly and fully indifferent — and that the transformation still to be accomplished in me will have to be the Lord's work, not mine. What I can and must do, of course, is to cooperate with the Lord's transforming work in me. He has not forced himself upon me in the past, and he will not bring to perfection the good work he has begun in me without my wholehearted assent.

We cannot doubt that Ignatius would agree with this clarification. He presents the "Principle and Foundation" at the very beginning of the *Spiritual Exercises*, not as a precondition for making the retreat but as the very work to be accomplished in the retreat itself. The *Exercises* are the means to bring us to the centering love of God and to the indifference to all created things, which the "Principle and Foundation" proposes as our ideal. Also, it is clear that God is the primary agent in the retreat. As Ignatius says in Annotation (Introductory Observation) #5: "It will greatly benefit the one making the retreat to enter upon the *Exercises* with a courageous heart and with generosity . . . in order that His Divine Majesty may make use of his person and all he possesses according to His most holy will." Hence "making ourselves indifferent" can only mean cooperating with the Lord in his work of transforming us.

Having made all these clarifications, we can now say that Ignatian indifference is indeed the "principle and foundation" of any genuine spiritual life. It is the goal toward which we are directed from the very beginning. Our growth in this indifference is the best sign that our life with God is indeed on the right track. It is also the key indicator that we are growing in that divine common sense of which we have been speaking. The more we come to see God as the be-all and end-all of our lives, and the more we see our other loves and gifts as subordinate to and as "means" toward this end, the more we possess the mind of Christ in our way of judging and acting day by day.

Our Eucharistic Life

Of all the means which the Lord has given us to achieve our end, the greatest by far, for those of us who are Catholics, is the eucharist. I recently had the privilege of giving a five-day seminar on discernment for a group in Canada. My co-presenter was a Protestant minister, a friend who, during his days as a missionary in the Philippines, had completed his doctorate at our Loyola School of Theology. His doctoral thesis was a comparison of the spiritualities of John Wesley — his denomination, the

Christian and Missionary Alliance, is rooted in the Methodist tradition — and Ignatius Loyola, both of whom give great value to what Ignatius calls "discernment." As it happened, virtually all the seminar participants were also Protestants from various traditions. Since I was celebrating Mass each day, I invited the participants to attend if they wished. Almost all of them did, and their experience was beautifully revealing to me.

In the first place, I realized that a number of them had never, or rarely, attended a Catholic Mass before. They had many questions about what Catholics believe about the eucharist, since for most of them the communion service, while part of their traditions, is only a memorial of the Last Supper. They were, however, genuinely interested in knowing what I believe. My attempts to explain my faith in the Real Presence of Jesus in the sacrament, and to explain what I understand a sacrament to be, made me realize anew what a tremendous gift my eucharistic faith is. This was reinforced by the second revealing aspect of my experience with them: many of them told me at the end of the week that the daily eucharist had been the high point of the whole seminar for them, even though they saw it with different eyes and from diverse faith perspectives.

What is this tremendous treasure we hold in our hands? Why has Catholic tradition always held that the eucharist is the center of our faith and the crown of our whole sacramental life? My experience in Canada led me to reflect that relatively few Catholics fully appreciate the treasure that we, God's earthenware vessels, contain in ourselves (2 Cor 4:7). For Catholics, the eucharist is indeed a memorial of the Last Supper and the Paschal Mystery, as the Protestants believe and as Jesus commands in the prayers of consecration. But it is a very special kind of memorial: it makes to be truly present, here and now, the very mystery of love it commemorates.

Christ Jesus is present in our midst today, under the appearances of bread and wine. He is, as the theologians put it today, a "sign in the strong sense." Most signs (like street signs, traffic lights, national flags) point to an independently existing reality. They are not themselves that reality. For example, if a truck destroys the street sign at the corner of your street, you don't ask what happened to the street. The street is still there; only the sign is missing.

By contrast, Jesus in the eucharist (and in all the sacraments) is a sign in the strong sense. That is, he embodies, makes present in and to the community, the very love of God that he symbolizes. If he were not there, God's love would not be there either. "No one can come to the Father except through me. . . . To have seen me is to have seen the Father" (Jn 14:6-9). We call this the mystery of faith, because it is virtually unique in our natural experience. Some human signs, particularly the act of making love in a good marriage, do go beyond being mere signs. They "realize," make real and deepen, the very love they symbolize. Of course, Christian matrimony is a sacrament too, and as such it symbolizes much more than the love of husband and wife alone. It makes Christ Jesus the third party, and the bond of unity, in any genuine Christian marriage.

These are deep and mysterious realities. But common sense is grounded on truth. We can only approach the eucharist sensibly if we have some feeling for what a sacrament is. We may not know or understand all the technical details of the theologians' explanations. But we do know that a sacrament is not just another reality in our world of sense experience. We do not understand the eucharist by subjecting the consecrated bread and wine to chemical analysis. At the same time, it is not magic, a way of manipulating physical reality to gain control over God and nature. This is what medieval magicians, like contemporary satanists, believed with their "hocus pocus" (a supposedly magical corruption of "*Hoc est corpus*," the first words of the consecration of the bread). The eucharist is God breaking into and transforming our world, not our gaining control of God and taking divine power into our hands.

How, then, does the sensible and sensitive Christian approach the eucharist? With a profound sense of mystery, first of all. Not magic, but mystery. We don't try to reduce God to the size of our own minds. We are aware that the reality symbolized is far more important than the symbol. Since it is God's symbol, we have to let God teach us the full meaning of the reality it symbolizes.

It is in the scripture that God gives us some important clues concerning this central mystery of faith.

The Lord tells us in John 6 us that he is the Bread of Life and no one can live who refuses to eat his flesh and drink his blood. So the eucharist is not primarily the reward for having lived a good life. Rather, it is the necessary condition for being able to live a good life. When we go down the aisle to communion, we are not saying that we are already holy. On the contrary, we are proclaiming to the world that we cannot be holy, live a good life, without Jesus. He came not for the well but for the sick, "not to call the virtuous, but sinners" (Mt 9:12-13). We proclaim by receiving him that we are the sick for whom he came, and that our only hope of healing is in him. To stay away from communion because we are "not worthy" would be like refusing to eat because we are suffering from malnutrition and cannot enjoy the food.

We will have more to say shortly about this problem of unworthiness. First, though, let us note that another important aspect of our eucharistic faith, as the church has always taught, is that the eucharist is the sacrament of Christian unity. Just as many grains form the one bread, and many grapes the one cup, so we, though many, are one in Christ Jesus. Or, as St. Paul puts it: "The fact that there is only one loaf means that, though there are many of us, we form a single body because we all share in this one loaf" (1 Cor 10:17).

Jesus is the sacrament of God's presence among us. What we refer to as the seven sacraments are particular aspects of God's presence to us in Jesus. Baptism, for example, symbolizes our reception of new life at the hands of Jesus. Confirmation symbolizes our being strengthened to live our faith as mature Christians. And, at the heart of all sacramentality, is the eucharist, the sacrament of the unity in love of all who belong to Jesus Christ. As the refrain of one of our best-known eucharistic hymns expresses it: "Oh, may we all one bread, one body be, through this blest sacrament of unity."

St. John, whose gospel is rich in symbolism, has a very striking way of bringing home to us this central meaning of the eucharist. At the Last Supper, precisely where we would expect John to give us the words of consecration, he narrates instead Jesus' washing of the feet of the disciples. From chapter 6, John's eucharistic faith is clear. Writing last, he knew of the accounts of its institution in the other evangelists and in Paul. Why, then, does he omit it in his own account of the Last Supper? Because, typically for John, he wants us to be puzzled, so we will be forced to look deeper. For John, the washing of the feet gives the real meaning of the eucharist: we are made one and we proclaim our unity precisely by our humble service of one another in imitation of Jesus. "You call me Master and Lord, and rightly; so I am. If I, then, the Lord and Master, have washed your feet, you should wash each other's feet. I have given you an example so that you may copy what I have done to you" (Jn 13:13-15).

In recent years we have reintroduced the ceremony of the washing of the feet in the Holy Thursday liturgy. It is a beautiful addition, because it makes real for the community the symbolism of Jesus' action. We must, however, use good sense in explaining the meaning of that symbolism. In Jesus' culture, washing the feet was not an act of humiliation. It was the ordinary gesture of hospitality in a dusty, semi-arid country, where people wore sandals. It would be similar, in the two cultures I know best, to offering newly-arrived guests a cold drink.

When Peter objects to the washing, what disturbs him is not that his feet are washed, but that it is Jesus who washes them. Ordinarily the servants would perform this service; only when the guests were important people did the master of the house do the washing himself. And this is precisely what Jesus wishes to say: Peter (and every disciple) is a very important person! There are no first-class and second-class citizens in the kingdom of God.

The eucharist is the symbol of Christian unity, and John is telling us that this unity is realized precisely in our mutual and humble service of one another. In my Philippine barrio, washing the feet seems to be an act of humiliation, and those washed are more embarrassed than the one washing! So I try to make Jesus' meaning clearer by washing the hands of the whole congregation. I first read the account of the incident (Jn 13:1-11), and then pause to wash the hands of all present, with the help of the barrio leaders. When we have finished, I read the ending of the gospel, where Jesus explains "what I have done to you" (13.13). And then I elaborate in my homily what the washing tells us about our eucharistic faith. This way of doing it seems to be beautifully effective with my barrio community. But the important thing, however we accomplish it, is to make the sacramental symbolism come alive.

Our Penitential Life

We spoke above of the eucharist as the medicine of the sick. I said that being "unworthy" is not a good reason to abstain from communion. Obviously, though, this statement needs clarification. Toward the middle of Chapter 2, in the section "Pauline Criteria of Authentic Growth," I mentioned that we need to distinguish between sin as malice and sin as sickness. The point there was that sin as malice — where there is deliberate bad will and we are not even trying to overcome our failings — is a sign that we are not growing in holiness. Such deliberate sin, if we are not truly sorry for it when we come to Mass, would render us unworthy to receive communion. We cannot approach the Lord as our Savior and Healer if we do not want to be healed and saved.

We must keep in mind, however, the church's constant teaching that, for grave sin, three elements are required: serious matter, sufficient reflection, and full consent. Impatience with a spouse or co-worker would not normally be serious or grave matter, whereas adulterous or murderous thoughts would be. But in the latter case, for grave sin there would also need to be sufficient reflection; that is, the adulterous thoughts do not just catch us off-guard or come suddenly into our minds. At that point they are merely temptations, and a thousand temptations do not make a single sin. All of us are tempted every day, although the specific temptations vary, depending on our personality and our circumstances. But even if these temptations persist to the point where we do have time to reflect that the action or thought in question is wrong, still we will not commit grave sin unless we freely and fully consent to what we see is contrary to God's will for us.

I think this question of full consent is, for committed, devout persons, the trickiest part of the church's teaching on grave sin. We often can find ourselves in the situation of Paul in Romans 7, where "I see the good and I want it, and yet I find myself doing the evil I do not want." This will happen particularly in areas where our instincts are very strong: sensuality, self-vindication, fear, and so forth. This is where the common sense of the friend of God is especially important. To begin with, we should be firmly convinced that the Lord desires our salvation even more than we do. God is not just sitting back and waiting to see whether we evaluate things correctly or confess properly. Therefore, we should simply express our sorrow as best we can, with whatever understanding we have of our own responsibility (our "full consent"). When we are doubtful whether, or to what degree, we consented to the evil thought or action, we should simply tell the Lord that we are sorry for our thoughts or actions as he sees them.

The fathers of the church often spoke of the sacrament of penance (or reconciliation, as we call it today) as the "sacrament of peace." If it is not productive of inner peace, something is wrong with the way we (or the confessor) are approaching it. That is why scrupulosity is not a virtue but a sickness: scrupulous people never come to peace. They confess the same sins over and over, always fearing that they have not confessed properly or have not made themselves understood by the confessor. Or they agonize over the precise degree of their consent to the temptations they have experienced. In either case, the peace of the sacrament, grounded in the supreme confidence with which Paul ends Romans 7 ("thanks be to God" our victory is certain "through Christ Jesus our Lord"), eludes them.

I said that scrupulosity is a sickness, and it can be a very painful one indeed. But scrupulous individuals often can help themselves by applying a good dose of common sense. They can realize and affirm that it is they (not the good God) who is torturing themselves. However difficult it may be to control the tortured feelings, they can firmly and resolutely entrust themselves to the mercy of God. Virtue, like sin, is not in the feelings but in the will. Even if their feelings of anxiety and guilt persist, they can make them occasions of grace by continually and insistently surrendering themselves to Christ, who died for love of them and who, by rising from the dead, conquered death and sin in them. If they find even this surrender impossible, they can at least be clear that their problem is not spiritual but psycho-emotional. Good sense dictates, as I often have to remind myself in my ministry, that we not try to cure psychological problems by moral or spiritual remedies.

Most of us, thank God, are not scrupulous. Since Vatican II, in fact, with its stress on the love of God and our call to lifelong growth, I find scrupulosity much less prevalent among Christians. What then does good sense dictate for the "ordinary" person, who can distinguish among full consent, doubtful consent, and no consent at all to the temptations we all encounter? We should be clear, first of all, that temptation is not sin. Jesus was tempted ("in every way that we are," Hebrews 4:15 says), though he never sinned. John of the Cross says that the more we grow in holiness, the more we will be tempted. Why? Because the devil has much more to gain by derailing a truly committed pray-er than by working on someone who is already in his camp. I have long felt that this is why we pray for the pope and the bishops in every eucharistic prayer: not because they are more privileged members of the church, but because they are more vulnerable to the attacks of the Evil One. The devil has much to gain if he can lead the pope astray, because of his position in the church and the many people who would be scandalized if he did wrong. As Jesus told Peter: "Satan, you must know, has got his wish to sift you all like wheat; but I have prayed for you, Simon, that your faith may not fail; and once you have recovered, you in your turn must strengthen your brothers and sisters" (Lk 22:31-32). So temptation is a normal part of Christian life; in fact, it will be more common, and more intense as we grow closer to the Lord.

The committed pray-er who possesses good judgment

can distinguish between free consent to temptation and doubtful consent. Actually, clear deliberate malice will be quite rare among those we are talking about, since they are truly in love with the Lord. What will be more common is the Romans 7 situation, where they find themselves doing the very things they hate. How culpable are they? At times it will be clear that they did not will the evil thought or deed: for example, when they are half asleep or over-whelmed by temptation despite a lengthy struggle to resist it. Such situations are humiliating and, as we saw in Chapter 2, they can also be truly humbling (in a good sense) if they bring us to a more radical and total depen-dence on the grace of Jesus.

This is also true in situations where we are doubtful whether, or to what extent, we consented to the temptation. Here too, persons of good sense, who have learned to trust the Lord, will simply tell him they are sorry for their failure as he sees it. We often cannot get, and we do not need, any greater clarity than that about our degree of guilt.

What about confession or the sacrament of reconcilia-tion? Like all the sacraments, it is an encounter with Christ Jesus in an important area of our life. In confession we encounter Christ as our Savior and our Healer. We have said enough already to see clearly that this is a crucial ele-ment in our experience of Jesus. That is why the church rec-ommends the sacrament of reconciliation as an integral part of any authentic Christian spirituality. Confession is necessary when there is deliberate grave sin. But it is also very helpful in the more common cases of doubtfully grave or clearly venial sin. We cannot say that confession is strict-ly necessary in these cases, because they can be forgiven in other ways: for example, by the penitential rite at the beginning of Mass, by a devout reception of the eucharist, or by a sincere act of contrition. Nonetheless, periodic reg-ular reception of the sacrament of reconciliation is very helpful for committed persons. It brings us face to face with Jesus as our healing and redeeming Lord. It keeps our eyes on the goal of transformation, so that we see these "small failings" not as trivial events but as blocks to being able to love as we are loved. Reconciliation opens us to the Spirit's transforming work in us.

Such a confession has traditionally been called a "confession of devotion," rather than a confession "of obligation." How often should we confess in this way? I find about once a month a good frequency, and this also seems to be the ideal in recent church documents. If we tend to be lax (for example, making excuses for every failing), it might be good to work against this laxity by confessing more frequently; if scrupulosity is our problem, it is probably wise to resist the tendency to be anxious by confessing less frequently. For most of us, though, once a month is probably a good norm.

How does one make a fruitful confession of devotion? I find it helpful, in the first place, to situate my sinfulness in the context of God's personal love for me, and not merely in the context of law. That is, I ask where or how I have most encountered the Lord since my last confession. I begin by "confessing" this encounter of love (as Augustine does in his classic *Confessions).* Then, since I am not obliged to give a whole laundry-list of sins — and since such a detailed catalogue is not, at least for me, productive of peace and of depth of experience — I focus on the one or two failings I feel most need healing at this time. In fact, in order to make my confession an act of discerning love, and not just of self-evaluation, I like to ask the Lord, when preparing to receive the sacrament, what he would like me to confess at this time.

The actual confession, then, might sound like this: "Bless me, Father, for I have sinned. My last confession was one month ago. During that time I have experienced God's love working through me especially in the lives of my directees. In the light of this, I feel that I have failed by being too self-centered in my ministry — by seeking to draw people to myself and not purely to the Lord." I might conclude by saying: "I am sorry for all my sins, but, in this confession, I particularly ask the Lord's healing for my self-centeredness."

I have recommended this approach to confession to many others. The beauty of it is that it situates my sinfulness in the context of God's personal love for me during the past month. It will never become routine or boring, because I will never encounter the Lord in precisely the same way from month to month. It is true that my Romans 7 failings may be monotonously repetitive, because they reflect my personality and my history. But those who trust their doctor are willing to return as long as their course of treatment takes. They do not feel they need a new illness to report every time they visit the doctor's office.

Communal and Personal Prayer

Friends often tell me that the practice of confession has almost died out in their parishes. This is, I think, a reaction to our Jansenist past, when people saw mortal sin everywhere and we believed that we had to confess before every reception of communion. The church has clearly rejected this pessimistic and rigoristic stress on the gulf between our radical sinfulness and God's unimaginable holiness. As we saw in Chapter 2, we already live the life of God by virtue of our baptism. Paul, in writing to the gentile Christians at Ephesus, tells them that they and the Jewish converts "are God's work of art, created in Christ Jesus to live the good life, as from the beginning he had meant us to live it" (3:10). The stress today, as in Paul, is not on our sinfulness but on our new life in Christ. We Christians are radical optimists.

The problem in our day, however, is that we seem to

have thrown out the baby with the bath water. In affirming our optimism, we can forget that we live in tension between the already and the not yet. We can forget, as Paul never did, that baptism is but the beginning of a lifelong process of transformation — that we still find the two laws of Romans 7 at war within us. The victory is indeed certain for those who persevere in hope and who cooperate by opening themselves to the Spirit at work in their lives. The approach to confession that I suggested above is one good way to cooperate with the Lord in our ongoing transformation. It may not be the only way, but it has been helpful to me and to many others to whom I have recommended it.

Another area where the baby/bath water syndrome seems to operate today is the practice of penance or mortification. In the past much popular (and some liturgical) piety saw penance or mortification as a means of pleasing God. Today we have the good sense to realize that God does not enjoy our suffering. We don't make God happy by making ourselves miserable. But again, the pendulum seems to have swung to the other extreme. While denying that mortification can be a means of pleasing God, we may have concluded that it has no place at all in the Christian life. In so doing we may have lost sight of its real value: not to please God, but to strengthen ourselves for the struggle of life.

As I see it, the human will is like a muscle. It is developed and strengthened only by exercise. Professional athletes submit themselves to rigorous programs of conditioning. They may — and I presume most do — find these workouts boring and exhausting, but they want to be in good shape when the real game takes place. This is precisely the purpose of mortification in the life of the committed Christian: it strengthens his or her will for the challenges involved in being a true disciple of Jesus. Paul even uses the athletic metaphor to explain his own ascetical life:

> All the fighters at games go into strict training; they do
> this just to win a wreath that will wither away, but we
> do it for a wreath that will never wither. . . . I treat my
> body hard and make it obey me; for, having been an
> announcer (i.e., having preached to others) myself, I
> should not want to be disqualified (1 Cor 9:27).

This is another area where good common sense is
important. We must see penance or mortification as a
means and not as an end. We don't do it for its own sake,
but in order to strengthen our wills to resist the devil's
attacks and to be firm in our commitment to Christ. Also,
we must choose those penances most suited to our own
personal weaknesses and to the challenges of our own
vocation. The weight-lifter and the long-distance runner
need to develop different muscles and a different type of
stamina, so they train differently. Similarly, each of us, as
athletes of Christ, must know the demands of our own particular vocation and our own areas of weakness. For those
who hate to eat, fasting is not a very good penance. They
might do better by forcing themselves to eat properly and
well, despite their distaste for doing so.

A healthy asceticism is an essential element in any personal program of spirituality. As St. Teresa says, in teaching
her sisters to pray in *The Way of Perfection*, the three pillars
of a good prayer life are humility, fraternal love, and mortification. Any spirituality not grounded on these three
essential prerequisites is an illusion and a fraud. Teresa was
one of the most practical, down-to-earth saints in the history of the church; her good sense still rings true four hun-
dred years later.

We have spoken about Teresa's other two pillars,
humility and fraternal love, in earlier chapters of this book.
I have also discussed, especially in Chapter 4, what it

means to view formal prayer, and the contemplation which is its normal culmination, from a common-sense perspective. We saw that God begins the courtship; as we grow in prayer, God gradually does more and more and we do less and less. It was also clear that we should judge our prayer by the difference it makes in our lives (Teresa's stress on fraternal love is most relevant here) and not by the beautiful, ecstatic experiences which may occur during the prayer itself. All of these insights are indicative of a sound common sense at work in our personal prayer lives. What we can now add are a few practical footnotes.

First of all, we should maintain a healthy balance between communal and personal prayer. We need both, since we come before God both as unique individuals and as members of the Body of Christ. As many saints have stressed, notably St. Cyprian and St. Teresa of Avila in their treatises on the Lord's Prayer, from the very beginning Jesus taught us to say "*Our* Father" — not "my" but "our." Vatican II gives great importance to the communal, ecclesial dimension of our encounter with God.

Because communities are human, they can drag us down as well as lift us up. It can be that the parish's or prayer community's way of acting and relating (or not relating) makes it impossible for us to worship God. In such a situation, we might be well-advised to search for a more congenial community. But the dying to self, and the adjustment to other ways of acting and reacting entailed by any community worship, can be an important part of our purifying process of transformation. Like everyone else, I find some aspects of common worship distracting and unhelpful. Others never (or rarely) do things exactly as I would do them. Still, I find this difficult experience valuable — and not only because it is a good penance. It reminds me that I am not there only to meet my own needs. What is not helpful to me may be helpful to others. I should be there for them, and not just for myself.

In group retreats today it is fashionable to ask the retreatants to do a written evaluation at the end. In fact, the same practice is followed in one of the faculties where I teach. What is most revealing is that what one retreatant or student finds especially helpful is precisely what another criticizes. Some find my conferences too long; others find the length just right; others find them too short. Again, I seem to be famous (as my readers have also commented many times) for the stories I tell about my family to illustrate the points I am making. Many say this helps them make concrete the principles we are talking about and apply them to their own lives. That, of course, is my purpose. But it seems there is always someone who finds the practice irritating. As one recent retreatant put it bluntly: "I was disappointed that he spent so much time talking about his family. It would have been much more helpful if he talked less about them and more about spirituality."

At the very least, such comments are good for my humility. But I see a deeper meaning here. It is impossible to please everyone, painful as that truth is. As the old proverb has it, "one person's meat is another's poison." Or, as my mother (!) used to say: "'Every man to his own taste,' the old lady said as she kissed the cow." Pastorally, what I or any minister of Christ must do is to be sensitive to which modes of presentation are helpful to most of my hearers. I am there not to glorify myself but to help them. I hope the ones I don't reach will be helped by some other director or teacher with another style. I must, of course, "speak the truth in love" as I see it. But good sense requires that I do not expect to please everyone or meet everyone's needs. Even Peter and Paul had their adherents; Paul had to remind the Corinthians (1 Cor 1:12-13; 3:5-6) that he and Cephas and Apollos were mere instruments of the one Messiah and the one Message, Jesus Christ.

We have spoken much about the communal dimension of our prayer lives, since this is an aspect about which I have not said much in earlier books. Before ending this chapter, though, let us return to our basic point, that what is needed is a healthy balance between the personal and the communal in our prayer. We Christians are not isolated individualists. But neither are we simply parts of a bigger whole. Christ died for each of us personally. Like a good mother, God loves and cares for each of us in our uniqueness. When all is said and done, we each need to write our own "gospel," our own faith story. That means we need time and space to relate to God personally, just as every child needs quality time with his or her parents. This does not deny the child's place in the family, but it does mean that he or she is not just a cog in the family wheel.

As I grow older I marvel — more accurately, I find it mind-boggling — that God can care for me personally in a world of five billion people, and not only for me, but for each of the other five billion. Many agnostics find this impossible to believe. I must admit I don't understand it any more than they do. But I know by experience that it is true. Good sense demands that I not deny or doubt my own experience of God's ways. It also demands that I respond in kind to God's utterly personal love for me. When all is said and done, that is what prayer is all about.

Chapter 6

God's Work and Good Sense

In a retreat which I gave recently, one of the retreatants observed that the *Spiritual Exercises* seem to be very individualistic. It is a comment I have heard before, particularly from those who are involved in work for social justice or reform of social structures. I can understand the point they are making: Ignatius' primary concern does seem to be the conversion and transformation of the individual person making the retreat. However, the same comment could be made about Jesus' ministry of formation in the gospels. Given the short span of his public life — about three years, as far as we can tell — he does seem to spend a surprising amount of time forming a very small circle of disciples.

Like Jesus himself, however, Ignatius sees this personal process of conversion as producing the fruit of a life of apostolic service. The disciples in the gospels are "to go out and bear fruit, fruit that will last" (Jn 15:16). Having been strengthened himself, Peter is to strengthen his sisters and brothers. Jesus sees the small seed that he has planted in the hearts of these few disciples as growing into a great tree, whose branches extend to every corner of the earth. Similarly, Ignatius sought the conversion and sanctification of his retreatants not merely for their own individual good, but in order that they might be "instruments shaped to the hand of God" — apt instruments to accomplish the Lord's work in the world. The great questions of the second week of the *Spiritual Exercises* are: What have I done for Christ? What am I doing for Christ? What shall I do for Christ?

Our concern today for the reform and transformation of social structures is one of the distinctive marks of contemporary Christianity. It is not, however, entirely new; in fact, the great saints of every age have been preoccupied with the social reform of the institutions of their times. To mention just a few, we can cite Benedict, Bernard, Catherine of Siena, Teresa of Avila, Thomas More — to say nothing of great Protestant figures like Martin Luther and John Wesley. In our time, however, we have new tools of analysis, like scientific sociology and social philosophy. Karl Marx was a pioneer here, a more scientific thinker than the doctrinaire Marxism of Lenin and Stalin might lead us to suspect. While much of Marx's social philosophy is outdated and erroneous, he did pose questions concerning the relationship of the person to society that still preoccupy Christian philosophers like Pope John Paul II.

If Ignatius were living today, I believe he would take these questions very seriously in forming apostles, men and women for others (as the great Fr. Pedro Arrupe expressed it), who are apt instruments of Christ in our time. I also believe, though, that he — and, more important, Jesus himself — would insist that social transformation cannot happen, and would be fruitless even if it did, unless the persons who make up the society are personally converted to Christ. As long as we believe in human freedom and personal responsibility, we cannot believe (as Marx seemed to) that changing social structures alone can make for a just and loving society. Structural change is certainly desirable, insofar as it creates a climate in which each person can grow to the limits of his or her own potential and generosity. But the idea that good structures will make for good citizens is utopian, to say the least. The cynicism that infects many democratic societies today is proof enough of this: "What is the point of voting? All politicians are alike. All we get are unfulfilled promises and gridlock." In countries that have experienced dramatic structural change, like Russia in 1917 or China in 1949 or the Philippines in 1986, the same cynicism soon resurfaces.

The view I am defending here is that Jesus' vision and approach are still relevant today. Personal conversion and transformation, effected by the grace of God with our cooperation (in the ways described in Chapters 2, 4 and 5), are as fundamentally necessary today as they were in Jesus' day. That is one thing we have learned from the tremendous social upheaval, in theory and in practice, of the past century. At the same time, it is also clear, as John Donne wrote, that "no man is an island." Our lives are inescapably social. The church is essentially a community, formed by the Spirit and preserved by mutual love and service. Like Magdalene on Easter (Jn 20:17-18), and like Peter and James and John on Tabor (Mt 17:1-9), all Christians who have seen the Lord must return to Jerusalem — to our ordinary lives and to the communities in which we live them. As Vatican II makes clear in "The Church in the Modern World," we can keep the Lord only by sharing him with others.

God's Work

If our life with God necessarily involves a reaching out to others, if contemplation must fructify in action, what can common sense (the common sense of God) teach us about the integration of these two poles of our life of faith? The most important lesson, and the real reason why contemplation must precede Spirit-led action, is that the world is God's and its salvation is his project. In fact, central to

Ignatius' apostolic spirituality in the sixteenth century was the conviction that God is already, and always, at work in the world. Apostles do not go into the world merely to share their experience of the Lord with others. They do indeed go to give, but they also go to receive. God is already in the world. It is not enough that we wash the feet of others. We must also allow them to wash our feet. "If I, then, the Lord and Master, have washed your feet, you should wash each other's feet" (Jn 13:14).

Underlying this mutuality of giving and receiving is the realization that the process of transforming the world begins and ends, and is sustained throughout, by the God and Father of Jesus, not by us. Jesus makes this beautifully clear in the Last Supper discourse: "The words I say to you I do not speak as from myself: it is the Father, living in me, who is doing this work" (Jn 14:10; see also 14:31). In this passage Jesus is speaking of himself and his work in the world. But he goes on to say: "I tell you most solemnly, whoever believes in me will perform the same works as I do myself; he will perform even greater works, because I am going to the Father" (14:12). Then he uses the famous image of the vine and the branches to insist that the fruitfulness of the branches is totally dependent on the pruning of the divine vinedresser. He then goes on: "I am the vine, you are the branches. Whoever remains in me, with me in him, bears fruit in plenty; for cut off from me you can do nothing" (15:5). And again: "You did not choose me; no, I chose you, and I commissioned you to go out and bear fruit, fruit that will last" (15.16). So our fruitfulness is ultimately the Father's work, accomplished through the Son.

Jesus' priestly prayer in John 17 has always seemed to me to be his last will and testament. When a person is about to die, we discover what is really important to him or her. My own father, a man who was very careful about all the minutiae in his life, had only two concerns during his last days in 1973: his family and his faith. All the other details which had preoccupied him in life, like the tax records and the care of the house and the car, faded into insignificance. What about Jesus? As he comes to the end of his earthly life, only two concerns dominate his priestly prayer: the Father's will, and the well-being of his beloved disciples.

Jesus rejoices, first of all, that "I have glorified you on earth and finished the work you gave me to do." And that "I have made your name known to those you took from the world to give me. They were yours and you gave them to me" (Jn 17:4,6; see also verses 8 and 12). The disciples and the work of Jesus in forming them were the gift and the mandate of the Father. Now that Jesus has fulfilled the Father's will, he can look forward to his reward: "to glorify me with that glory I had with you before ever the world was."

The second concern of Jesus on the eve of his death is the fate of the disciples the Father has given him: "But now I am coming to you, and while still in the world I say these things to share my joy with them to the full" (17:13). Not only does he share his final word of loving concern with them, but he also looks beyond his death and departure and entrusts to the Father the completion of the good work he has begun in them: "I am not asking you to remove them from the world, but to protect them from the evil one. . . . Consecrate them in the truth; your word is truth" (17:15, 17). Moreover, he also remembers all of us down through the ages: "I pray not only for these [the first disciples], but for those also who through their words will believe in me. May they all be one, Father . . . in us, as you are in me and I am in you" (17:20-21).

As we go about our work, then, our fundamental conviction is that it is really God's project, and that the final responsibility for it is his. We have no reason to be anxious, or to be overwhelmed by the challenges of our present-day world or the pressures of our work. If we are overworked or overwhelmed, something is amiss in our way of viewing our mission. Either we find it difficult to say no (a problem I face); or we allow ourselves to be governed by the expectations of others, when God alone is the Master for whom we work; or we ourselves bite off more than we can chew. If I read Jesus' words correctly, there is no reason for his disciples to be burdened beyond their strength. This is true whether their mission is to raise a family, to run a business, or to pastor a parish. Each of these is (or should be) a vocation from God. Therefore, Jesus' words in John 14—17 concerning our radical dependence on and trust in his Father should apply in every human situation.

I do not mean to imply that this attitude of trusting discipleship, of being merely God's instrument, will always be easy to maintain or be clear in its concrete demands. That is why discernment is so important in our active lives. The devil will try to confuse us, seeking to persuade us very piously (as "an angel of light," Ignatius says) to take responsibility for more than we should. Other people will do the devil's work by weighing in with their opinions and adding their pressure concerning what we should or should not do. The only sane and sensible way to react, when it is not obvious that their ideas contradict God's will for us, is to bring their suggestions to prayer. We have to be able to become quiet and to see the problems and challenges from the perspective of the Master of the Vineyard.

This is precisely what we mean by discernment. It is an art, an acquired skill, which we learn by experience. I have written in some detail about the process in *Weeds Among the Wheat*. Suffice it to say here that it involves bringing all our problems and decisions to the Lord, in order to discover in prayer what he wishes us to do. This means being able to come to a listening quiet, surfacing the concerns of the moment, handing them over to the Lord for guidance, and then waiting patiently for him to show us his will. We know that he always speaks in peace and that turmoil or restlessness or a sense of crisis are never his voice. At the beginning of our lives as God's co-workers, a good director can help to interpret what the Lord is saying to us. As we mature, we ourselves will possess an ever greater sensitivity to his will, born of discerning love. At every stage of our life, however, the fundamental, bedrock attitude must be "that the One who began this good work in [us] will see that it is finished when the Day of Christ Jesus comes" (Phil 1:6). All is God's work. That was Jesus' way — and it must be ours, too.

God's Demands and Expectations

We have seen from the very beginning of this book that an anxious desire for perfection is not a healthy sign in our lives. It is the Lord who began the work in us, and it is he who will bring it to perfection in his own good time. Moreover, this is as true of our mission in the world as it is of our own personal sanctification. I encounter many committed persons who are greatly distressed by the state of the world today: the prevalence of abortion, the many broken marriages, the barbaric cruelty in Rwanda and Bosnia and Cambodia, the gulf between haves and have-nots, the destructive drug culture. These are indeed tragic realities, and the distress of my friends is quite understandable. But they have to be careful not to play God; that is, not to take all the problems of the world on their own shoulders. Ultimately, the solution to all of this is God's responsibility.

What, then, is our responsibility? What would the Lord like us to do about these tragedies? How would he like to work through us? There is much wisdom, I think, in the famous slogan of the Christopher movement: "It is better to light one candle than to curse the darkness." As I understand it, this means keeping our eyes open to what is happening in our own corner of the world and then responding to the needs that are right at our own doorstep. The communications explosion today is not an unmixed blessing, since it makes us aware, almost instantaneously, of what is happening everywhere. And once aware, we can feel somehow responsible — for Rwanda, for South Africa, for North Korea, for places we have never been and to which we never expect to go.

This can be a blessing if it leads us to pray for all peoples in need. At times, too, we may be able to do something; for example, we may influence our government or our employer in formulation of their policies toward Bosnia or South Africa. But we have to exercise our common sense, too. Aimless anxiety does not help the Bosnians, and it does not help us either. In fact, it could be the devil's way of paralyzing us so that we never do light our own candles in the small darkness where we actually live. We may miss what the Lord is asking us to do, because we are overwhelmed by all that needs to be done everywhere.

What can we say, then, about our own small darkness? About our own small corner of the world? All of us have our part of the vineyard to cultivate, a community or group of persons to whom the Lord sends us. How do we act as God's good stewards where we are placed? It may be a family, or an office staff, or (as in my case) a community of seminarians. Whatever the shape of our vineyard corner, the most important guiding principle is to deal with others as the Lord has taught us to deal with ourselves. As we have seen, this means combining patience with perseverance. God's basic "demand" is that we entrust our lives to him and learn to dance to his music.

When Jesus commands us to "love your neighbor as yourself" (Mt 22:39; also 19:19), he is really giving us two commandments wrapped up in one. I cannot reply to him: "Okay, Lord. I hate myself. Therefore, it is also acceptable to hate my neighbor." That is obviously not what Jesus means. We are obliged to love ourselves, and this means to accept ourselves as God accepts us. God loves the real person who is present here and now, but he also loves us for what we can be. God's world is in the process of becoming, and we are part of that process. This is why we must combine patience with perseverance: patient acceptance of who we really are at present, and patient acceptance, too, of our slow process of growth, with perseverance in opening ourselves to this growth as long as we live. When we fail, as we often do, we have to remind ourselves of the need to be both patient and persevering. Teresa of Avila has said that the saint is not the person who never falls, but the person who gets up every time she does fall. That, as my own experience tells me, takes real humility. Our wounded pride urges us to discouragement and defeatism.

If I am correct in my understanding of Jesus' command to love ourselves, then it is clear what loving our neighbor as ourselves must mean. Whether that neighbor is the child I am raising, or the seminarian I am forming, or the co-worker at the next desk, I must bring the same combination of patient acceptance and persevering hope to our dealings. I must be clear that each person belongs to the Lord and not to me. Insofar as I do make any "demands," they must be the Lord's demands and not mine. St. John of the Cross, in his classic discussion of the three great enemies of spiritual growth (*The Living Flame of Love*, III, #29-67), says they are the devil, oneself, and the spiritual director! And by far the greater part of his discussion is devoted to the spiritual director. John says that many, perhaps most, directors do harm by trying to make their directees carbon copies of themselves. If they have found profit in a certain style of prayer or a certain spirituality, they try to force their directees into the same mold.

Since I spend much of my life giving spiritual direction, I try to reread John's discussion every year — to keep myself honest. But I think what he says would apply equally well to anyone who is doing God's work in the world. We should not impose our standards, or our way of seeing, on others. This does not mean, however, that we take a purely hands-off stance in our dealings with them, not, at least, if the Lord has somehow chosen us as instruments in forming them. John of the Cross says the good director has a real role to play in helping directees interpret their experience, in explaining to them the basic demands of gospel discipleship, in challenging or encouraging them as their current situation may demand. In other words, the director (or the parent or the confidant) must be sensitive to the Lord's demands on, and expectations for, this person at this moment in his or her life. Maybe that is why, in John's experience, few persons fulfill the director's role properly. The good instrument of the Lord must also be a person of listening prayer, shaped to the hand of God.

God's Pace

It may sound strange, but I often thank the Lord that I am not God. When I read passages like Matthew 5:43-45 on loving one's enemies and on being like God "who causes his sun to rise on bad men as well as good," I realize how much more tolerant God is than I am. Especially when I am weak and sinful, I know that if I were God, I would have given up on myself long ago. But God revealed himself to Moses as "Yahweh, a God of tenderness and compassion, slow to anger, rich in kindness and faithfulness; for thousands he maintains his kindness, forgives faults, transgressions, sin" (Ex 34:6-7). That is why I am deeply grateful that God is God and not I.

As I grow older, it is easier to be more spontaneously sure of God's kindness and fidelity in my life, as well as in the lives of those I serve. I feel serenely confident now, because of my long years of experience, that God will not give up on me or on them. What still remains a challenge for me is to accept God's pace in accomplishing his will in us. I have a friend who, I like to say, is the slowest person alive. His sentences are filled with long pauses. And I, being much quicker, am always tempted to move the conversation along. Another good friend has said to me more than once: "You know, you should not finish his sentences for him." And I reply: "Yes, I know. But I'm visiting for only a few days, and I was hoping we could move on to another topic before I leave!"

The second friend is right, of course. I know I have to be patient and let my slow-speaking friend move at his own pace. I tell the story now because, as I have often said to others, the only person slower than my friend is God. As I grow older, I think I understand why. My friend's slowness may be attributed to personality and temperament. With the Lord, I believe it is because he thinks in a much vaster time-frame than ours. After all, God has been shaping the world for billions of years. It took millions of years to prepare the human race for the coming of the Messiah. By contrast, you and I have to accomplish our goals in a mere seventy years. We have, understandably, a sense of urgency about solving our problems and completing our work that God does not have.

How liberating it is if our life of contemplation brings us closer to seeing things from the Lord's eternal perspective. There are days, of course, when I lose this divine perspective and find God frustratingly slow. But, more and more often, God's common sense prevails. I cannot really imagine yet, and will not be able to understand fully until I die, what it means to see persons and events in the light of eternity. It is a joy, though, to get some hint of it. And it helps me to be much more accepting of God's pace in dealing with the world and with the people I direct. I realize that I will understand my part in their lives, and the meaning of these few years that I journey with them, only when I meet them on Judgment Day and we — they and I — can see the whole picture.

Another insight from my philosophy of science background has helped me here. When we look at the heavens on a clear night, some of the most distant stars are so far away that, by the time we see them tonight, they have already gone out of existence — and this despite the fact that their light has been travelling toward us at a speed of 186,000 miles per second! It boggles the mind to think how distant they must be. We cannot even begin to imagine the immensity of God's universe. How then could we expect to understand the full story of one human being, on a single planet, circling one small star known to us as the sun? We would never pretend to grasp the point of a play from a single brief incident in the first act. It would be rather foolish to complain, on the basis of this one dramatic moment alone, that the playwright's artistic pace was too slow!

God's Sense of Humor

Fortunately for us, the Divine Playwright has a good sense of humor. God hears foolish complaints like this all the time without striking the critics dead. God knows that we are very slow learners. And God has been committed from the very beginning of creation to work with us at our pace. That is why, when people are distressed to discover their own human weakness and their slowness to respond to God's love, I have to ask them: "Who is disturbed by your sinfulness? Is it the Lord, or is it just you?"

This happens frequently in the first week of the *Spiritual Exercises*, when the grace the retreatants are seeking is to see and accept themselves as God sees and accepts them. I usually ask them, as a means to this grace, to do a profile of themselves, listing everything they think God likes and dislikes in them. Then, as described in Day Two of *Vacation With the Lord*, I ask them to rank the likes and the dislikes: that is, to guess which points the Lord likes and dislikes most.

This is not an easy exercise. I have described the grace we seek as "standing naked before the Lord." But it is, if done well, very liberating. For, after doing the profile, the retreatants have to bring it to the Lord in prayer — and ask him to confirm it or revise it or add to it. The grace, after all, is to see ourselves as God does not as we think God sees us (the point of the profile itself). We have to listen and let the Lord speak. Why is this liberating? Because almost always sincere pray-ers find that the Lord is much more tolerant than they are. When I ask them who is disturbed by their failings, God or themselves, they discover in prayer that it is they who are upset. The Lord seems to be smiling and saying: "I have known you from your mother's womb. I am not surprised by your foolishness and weakness. That is precisely what I committed myself to when I called you to my life. You are surprised, disappointed to discover how foolish you are, but not I!"

The Lord's sense of humor is gentle and healing. He does not cut our legs out from under us by making fun of us. On the contrary, he teaches us to find peace in being able to laugh at ourselves. After all, if the Lord loves me in my stupidity, what do I have to fear? But is it right to call this tolerant acceptance God's "sense of humor"? I think so. P. G. Wodehouse, my favorite human humorist, was once criticized by a famous Irish playwright (J. M. Synge, I believe) for being "the performing flea of the English language." It was meant as an insult: Wodehouse had a real gift for language, but he used it to produce irrelevant, frothy trivialities. The implication was that Synge himself, in his plays, went to the very heart of the human tragedy.

How did Wodehouse respond? In the course of a long life of ninety-three years (1881-1975) he wrote more than ninety books. Each of the Penguin reprints contains, on the first page, a quote which seems to be Wodehouse's answer to Synge: "I believe there are two ways of writing novels. One is mine, making a sort of musical comedy without music and ignoring real life altogether; the other is going right deep down into life and not caring a damn."

Synge, whom I liked very much at an earlier point when my life seemed deep and tragic, went "right deep down into life." It would perhaps be unfair to say he did not care a damn. But I think Wodehouse means that the tragic writers can leave us desolate and hopeless and despairing. They don't seem to care what happens to us after we plumb the depths of despair. By contrast, Wodehouse seeks with his gentle irony to help us to smile at ourselves, sometimes through our tears — and in so doing to gain strength to go on living the human comedy. Thus he does not really "ignore real life altogether." It would be more accurate to say that he looks at real life from a more detached standpoint — helping us to see the follies and the cruelties of ordinary life as but parts of a play that does come out happily in the end.

I would like to say that Wodehouse helps us to see human frailty in the light of eternity. The problem is that he does not give a religious meaning to our comical situation. Even his ecclesiastical characters — the naive young cleric shocked by his encounter with real love and real life, or the blustering bishop dominated by his wife, the "bishopess" — are themselves part of the human comedy of errors. Wodehouse does not venture into the realm of theology and spirituality. And yet my love for his writing is clearly because he speaks to me of the divine sense of humor. I hear Wodehouse's voice in Jesus' reply, when Peter says: "Lord, why can't I follow you now? I will lay down my life for you." The Lord responds to him: "Lay down your life for me? I tell you most solemnly, before the cock crows you will have disowned me three times" (Jn 13:37-38). There is tragedy here, but there is also that gentle irony which characterizes John's whole gospel. Peter does not know what he is really saying, but Jesus does. He rebukes Peter, but not rudely or angrily. The day will come, Jesus seems to be saying, when Peter will realize how silly his impulsiveness is. And the day also will come when Peter will realize that he spoke the truth, but in a way that he himself did not understand at the time.

The same gentle irony is captured by Francis Thompson's "fondest, blindest, weakest" in "The Hound of Heaven". We are foolish beings, but the Lord knew that from the beginning. He committed himself to us in our foolishness. And he works to shape something beautiful from the very unpromising raw material that we are. The day will come when Peter will "strengthen his brothers and sisters", and when Francis Thompson will see his very drug addiction as the opening to grace and glory in his life. If I guess correctly, P. G. Wodehouse has already discovered the divine meaning of his human comedy.

Meanwhile this gentle God of ours does have to chastise us at times, but even this is for our healing. Much of the time God waits and smiles indulgently, careful not to "break the crushed reed, nor put out the smoldering wick, till he has led the truth to victory" (Mt 12:20, quoting Is 42:3-4). If our contemplation has brought us to the common sense of God, we should reflect in ourselves the Lord's patience and persevering love — and healing sense of humor.